GEORGE FIELDING ELIOT

HOUR OF TRIUMPH

REYNAL & HITCHCOCK, NEW YORK

THIS COMPLETE EDITION IS PRODUCED IN FULL COMPLIANCE WITH THE GOVERNMENT'S REGULATIONS FOR CONSERVING PAPER AND OTHER ESSENTIAL MATERIALS.

PRINTED IN THE UNITED STATES OF AMERICA
BY THE CORNWALL PRESS, CORNWALL, N. Y.

Major G

HOUR OF TRIUMPH

Other Books by George Fielding Eliot

BOMBS BURSTING IN AIR

THE RAMPARTS WE WATCH

(with R. Ernest Dupuy)

IF WAR COMES

TO
LITTLE JOHNSTON

INTRODUCTION

In 1938, I wrote a book on the problems of American national defense entitled "The Ramparts We Watch."

That book was based on the belief that there existed both in Europe and in Asia a reasonable balance of power, and that the security of the United States could best be assured by the maintenance of powerful offensive armaments based largely on sea and air strength, coupled with a foreign policy of complete freedom of action.

The possibility of finding security in such a policy vanished when the collapse of France destroyed the balance of power in Europe, and, in its results, in turn destroyed the balance of power in Asia. When France went down, the involvement of this nation in the struggle against totalitarianism became instantly inevitable.

We have now been fighting for two years. We have fought a defensive war and a war of preparation, followed by limited offensives as our power increased. We are passing to the all-out offensive as this book is written. There seems no question that, with our Allies, we have a sufficient preponderance of strength to be victorious. But from now on the chief burdens of the war will be borne by Americans, as they have already been borne in turn by Chinese, by Britons, and by Russians. When victory is won, we shall have poured out our full share of blood, sweat and tears—and in the military sense we shall be more powerful than ever before in our history.

The course of the war will be profoundly affected by how

we think now about what will happen when it is won. The shape of the victory will be the shape of the events which bring victory to pass. Those events will not be altogether military; they will be in part political, in part economic. Their character will in large part depend on what we Americans think we are fighting for, and what we now begin to think and do about the use to which we shall, with our Allies, try to put the victory when we have won it.

The agencies and organizations which we of the United Nations will use in seeking to achieve our common aims after victory, will probably be developed during the course of the war. They will be essential instruments of cooperation both to win victory and to make use of it. Of greatest importance is the fact that, the more such agencies are developed now while war's necessities bind us all together, the greater will be the opportunity for the growth of that mutual confidence and good will, born of working and fighting and living together, which must be the foundation of any post-war edifice of international cooperation. So, and so only, may the true spirit of coalition be born.

A book about the fruits of victory cannot, therefore, merely concern itself with what may happen after victory has been attained. It must consider the present state of the war, and of public opinion; it must consider the probable course of the war, and the means by which victory seems likely to be won. Only thus can we come to any conclusion, even a tentative and provisional conclusion, as to what may be possible thereafter in the way of making use of victory in the service of mankind. We shall have our hour of triumph: but its worth to us and to our children will be measured by the use we make of it before the opportunities it affords have slipped away.

This book is written in the profound conviction that an early recurrence of the present holocaust will inevitably mean either the utter collapse of our civilization, or the establishment of a world-wide tyranny under which human rights and liberties will perish from the earth. It therefore seeks to examine the conditions under which victory may be attained, and the practical possibilities of reaping from that bloody harvest the fruits of a lasting peace.

Both in the winning of victory, and in the reaping of its fruits, the chief responsibility will, from this time forward, be borne by the people of the United States. No greater responsibility and no more splendid opportunity has ever come to any people since the dawn of history, than comes now to Americans as their hour of triumph draws nigh.

GEORGE FIELDING ELIOT.

CONTENTS

MAPS

1. THE PEOPLES' WAR

WE ARE ENGAGED in the most terrible war of all time.

It is terrible because it is both total war and global war. It is doubly terrible because it is the last total and global war which our civilization can hope to survive.

It is terrible because, though military victory is no longer in doubt, there are the gravest doubts as to whether the victors will find themselves prepared to reap the fruits of victory—the only fruits which could justify the cruel sacrifices of the war: the establishment of a just and lasting peace.

We of the United Nations stand now on the threshold of the great offensives which should bring us military victory. If we know not only how to gain that victory, but how to use it when the hour of triumph is at hand, our dead will not have died in vain. If we fail in either task, civilization as we know it will perish, as Graeco-Roman civilization perished fifteen centuries ago. The Dark Ages will come again.

We are fighting for the greatest stake for which men have ever fought: nothing less than the survival of freedom and human rights on all this earth, as against their extinction for centuries, perhaps forever.

It is not the liberty or enslavement of a single people which is now in question, but the whole of the gains—gains both social and political—that all men who have fought and died for liberty have ever won. The great struggle against the authoritarian concept of government began as the darkness of the Middle Ages began to pass away, began with Magna Carta and the Swiss Cantons, continued down the centuries as our forefathers and the forefathers of many another people now fighting at our side wrestled in their own way and according to their own lights with their particular tyrants. They fought for freedom, and all that freedom brings.

"Lance and sword and tumult, steel and gray goose wing,
Wrenched it, inch and ell and all, slowly from the king."

The English Civil War, the rise of the Dutch Republic, the American Revolution, the French Revolution, the progress of constitutional reform in the British Isles, the growth of the great free Dominions of the British Commonwealth of Nations, the cementing of our own Union in the fires of the Civil War, the Russian Revolution, the birth of the Republic of China, these were the milestones of this great march of humanity upward into the light.

But the world was growing smaller all the while; nations were becoming more and more dependent on one another as the demands of industry grew more varied, as international trade increased in volume, as the steamship, the airplane, the cable, and the radio abolished ancient restrictions of time and distance and made it less and less possible for a free state with a free economy to exist side by side with a slave state with a slave economy.

Almost a century has passed since Abraham Lincoln said: "This nation cannot exist half slave and half free." America had grown too small for two utterly opposite systems of life to exist within it side by side. Now it is the world which has grown too small, and we must face the fact—and all the grim implications of the fact—that this world cannot exist half slave and half free. Four years of civil war was the result of failure to accept, and to find a peaceful solution for the inexorable problem which Lincoln then stated; two world wars have been the result of failure to accept, and to find a peaceful solution for the equally inexorable problems which must be solved today if our civilization as we have known and built it through the centuries is to endure.

Now we are engaged in the second of those wars. It is a war which will test the ability of the human race, with all its intelligence, with all its courage, with all its scientific and social and spiritual progress, to find a means by which it may exist without either destroying itself, or becoming subject to the rule of a single tyranny.

The final testing ground will not be the battlefield. It will not be the council chamber. The Civil War was not won when Lee and Johnston surrendered the remnants of their gallant armies. It was not won when the Fourteenth Amendment abolished slavery, its ostensible cause. It was won only when the Southern States again took their places in the Union, when their Senators and Representatives sat in Congress, and above all when all Americans, North and South, accepted in their hearts as well as in their minds the living fact of an indestructible and permanent Union of all the States of this Nation, now and forever.

As it was with the War between the States, so it will be with this War between the Nations. It will not be won when the Allied armies have paraded in triumph through the Brandenburger Tor and down Unter den Linden. It will not be won when the last embers of Japanese resistance have been smothered by the hail of bombs and the Rising Sun has sunk back into the obscurity from which it arose to run its dreadful course across the skies. It will not be won when the peace treaties have all been signed, sealed and delivered, however wisely they may be drawn and however noble and unselfish the spirit which animates their authors. It will be won only when free men and women everywhere on this planet have accepted, not only in their minds but in their hearts, the fact that peace is indivisible, that it can be had only at a price, and that every one of us must pay a little part of that price and go on paying it for the inestimable privilege of living in a free and peaceful world. It will be won only when the United Nations has become as unquestionably a permanent and living fact as the United States has now become.

What is meant by "United Nations"? Fundamentally, a union of peoples bound together by a common interest and a common purpose. Armies can make such a union possible, but they cannot create it. Governments can prepare and sign treaties, but they cannot create a union that will be any more permanent than the Covenant of the League of Nations. Only peoples can do that—peoples who are resolved on peace in their time and in their children's time, peoples facing realistically the need for peace and the cost of its maintenance, and preferring to pay that cost day by day to the alternative of another war in twenty or thirty years.

It has been said that this is a peoples' war, and so it is, more truly a peoples' war than any which has ever been fought. It is the nature of total war that it is fought by whole peoples, that its weapons strike as cruelly at the civilian at home, at the woman and the child, as they strike at the armed soldier on the firing line, and that victory demands the utmost in effort from every member of the community, whether by fighting or by labor. On the general realization of this fact rests what hope there may be for a peoples' peace. No other can have any permanence, save the peace of annihilation or the peace of enslavement.

Once there was a general peace throughout the world as it was known to the ancients—the Mediterranean world. That peace was known as the Pax Romana. It came when all the other nations were slaves to Rome, and it was enforced by Roman mercenaries. We are fighting now to prevent the establishment of another peace like that, which future historians might come to call the Pax Germanica.

Once there was a period of comparative peace which lasted just a hundred years—1815 to 1914. It is generally known as the Pax Britannica, not because the world was enslaved by Britain, but because Britain held the central position in the balance of power on which that peace depended. There were wars during that time, but they were wars of limited extent and duration, because there was always a strong body of neutrals, generally led by Britain, which succeeded in preventing the spread of wars and keeping them within such bounds that they did not threaten the general political or economic structure of the world. There is much of instructive interest in the Pax Britannica, as I shall hope to demonstrate. But the world has grown too small for the balance of power system, and there have been no strong neutrals in the last two wars.

Since we will not have peace by single domination, and since we can no longer have it by the balance of power, there remains only one way in which we can have it—by common agreement among the peoples of the world, or the law-abiding majority among them.

Any peace established by such an agreement will last just as long as the peoples who establish it continue to place its preservation above individual, party and national ambitions and disputes. If our world can know a generation which has been born, lived, thrived and passed away without having known the blight of war, or perhaps even two or three such generations, there will be new foundations, new temples, new hope. More than that we dare not seek to assure with our feeble hands, our dim intellects, our limited vision.

To begin with, of course, we must win this war. That is the essential preliminary to any hope at all of a better world. But let us all see clearly what we are fighting for, and we shall win more quickly and at less cost. The men who won the war of the

American Revolution knew what they were fighting for. Basically, they were fighting for an ideal—liberty. That ideal was not unmixed with self-interest, of course, but whatever the social and economic causes of that war, it is fair to say that the common man who bled and froze and died in the Continental armies was inspired by a fierce and unshakable belief "that these United Colonies are, and of right ought to be, free and independent States." In a vague way, most of them knew that sometime, somehow, those States would have to be united in a single Nation, that some sort of Constitution would have to be created once independence was theirs. They knew the broad general principles which that Constitution would have to be designed to uphold. Many of them had more definite ideas about what it should contain; but they were not fighting for those details, they were fighting for the central idea of independence. They followed that bright banner to victory.

Today most of the men who are bleeding and fighting and dying under the flags of the United Nations, on battlefronts scattered all over this world, have, up to this time, been fighting *against* something rather than *for* something. They are fighting to destroy a danger rather than to realize an ideal. But in their hearts most of them cherish an ideal—the ideal of home and loved ones, of the coming time when they shall return victorious, to live in their own lands with their own people, at peace and unheeding the rumble of distant drums. As with the fighting men, so with the people at home, whose united effort is so essential a part of the great total effort of total war. In their hearts, too, is the one shining hope—the end of the war, the return of their absent ones, the re-uniting of families, the healing of wounds, and the happy days of peace beneath the skies of the homeland.

In a word—peace.

But peace is not altogether a matter of ideals, any more than liberty was in 1776. If you will read carefully the list of complaints against King George III which forms part of the Declaration of Independence, you will find many substantial charges of social and economic character, as well as the high ideals which are embodied in the Preamble. The men who made and led the War of the American Revolution were determined to be free of an odious tyranny, not only because it was revolting to their principles, but also because it was strangling their prosperity. It is when ideals and self interest march hand in hand that men may not only be roused to action, but will be most likely to continue their allegiance to the ideal which has been their inspiration, and whose enthronement has contributed to their welfare.

We have need, then, of what may be called a practical idealism: one which will neither lose sight of its purpose nor forget the reasons why that purpose must be accomplished; one which can appeal alike to the hearts, the minds and the spirits of our people, and of the hundreds of millions of people in other lands, without whose support the ideal of peace is unattainable.

Perhaps it may turn out that this practical idealism, which harmonizes so well with the character, the spirit and the history of the American people, may be America's most important contribution to the task of building the new peace. On the idealistic side, most Americans are ready now to accept the necessity of doing something about peace when this war is won. For the moment, however, it remains in the minds of most an idealistic necessity. Not yet have most of us realized that it is also a practical necessity, not only to the world, not only to the nation, but to each of us individually, affecting all our hopes and all our futures.

2. PRACTICAL IDEALISM

WHAT IS GOING to happen to me—and mine—after the war?

Every American is asking that question, either openly or in the secret places of his heart. As to the outcome of the war we are no longer in doubt. We and our Allies are assured of victory. We do not yet know how long it will take, or what the cost will be, but we know that we are going to win. But we are in doubt, all of us, as to our futures—each as to his own, all of us as to the collective future of the nation and the world in which we live.

This uncertainty, and the evils which may spring from it, are quite generally recognized. Political leaders seek to reassure the public mind by promises of social legislation, unemployment insurance, bonuses for returning soldiers and sailors, housing programs. The great voices of industry speak of an era of expansion, jobs for all, pension and profit-sharing plans. Scientists paint glowing pictures of the coming glories of radio, television, aviation and all the other wonders on whose threshold we stand. Educators, labor leaders, farm experts, and all the rest have their promises for the future. It will be a splendid world, a splendid prospect for our surviving youth, still more so for those whom they shall in their turn beget. But there is a note of anxiety underlying these assurances.

For all of us are thinking the same thing—and instinctively we know the truth, even if we do not admit it to ourselves.

The truth is, that most of these promises can be fulfilled only on one condition.

That condition is—peace.

That is why peace is so important to all of us.

That is why we may speak of this peace, the peace that is to be, as the people's peace, for the people need it, and the people must create it, and only the people can guard and preserve it. It is the last chance of the people to be free, to build, to pursue happiness.

For all of us, this is an intensely personal problem, this peace.

It isn't just an abstract and virtuous hope, to which we automatically give lip service and never really do anything about. It isn't a matter which is the sole concern of statesmen, soldiers and professors, whose decisions the rest of us must accept and make the best of. It isn't even a salvation to be attained through prayer, for is it not written that God helps those who help themselves?

Peace will not be ours without effort and sacrifice on the part of every one of us. It will not be our children's unless we begin now to teach them that it will cost them, in their turn, effort and sacrifice. It will not come to us automatically when victory is won. It will not remain with us unless human intelligence, using that gift of foresight which most particularly distinguishes it from animal intelligence, can realize that mankind must find a season of surcease from self destruction or perish from the earth.

It is of peace that each of us must first think in order to find an answer to that question—"What is going to happen to me and mine after the war?" For what is going to happen depends, first and foremost, on whether there is going to be, not only a temporary and uneasy cessation of hostilities as in 1918, but a real peace—an assured peace in whose endurance men can have confidence.

Until that is settled, nothing else counts very much. It has always been so.

Peace—in the sense of domestic peace, internal peace—has ever been the prerequisite of progress, of prosperity to human communities, since community life first began upon this earth, since the family first began to blend into the tribe and thus expand its horizons and its interests. No community has prospered until it has had peace within its own confines. This lesson man has had to learn and relearn, at every stage in his progress from tribe to village, from village to city, from city to nation.

Here in our own United States, we entered upon our longest unbroken era of progress and development when the Civil War ended our internal strife, and made us one Union, indivisible, stretching from sea to sea. Yet even during that time, we had sharp reminders of the need for community peace from our Far West, where many growing townships and counties and territories had to go through the same old process of trial and error in establishing local peace and security for their inhabitants, and in every case they began really to flourish and grow great only when this was done.

And in every case, all down the ages, the peace of every free community has been assured only by the use of force in the hands of the law-abiding majority. In every case, when the majority has been unable, or reluctant, or even hesitant to resort to force, there have been those who broke the peace to the despoiling of their neighbors. In every case where the majority has acted only sporadically, and under pressure, it has in the end cost far more in bloodshed and in treasure to suppress a lawlessness which foresight and prudence might have prevented altogether, or dealt with at little cost. In every case, the real solution has been found in the establishment of a reign of law, understood by all and supported by all, and backed by adequate and ready agencies of safe-guarded enforcement. Wherever this has not been the case, either the end has been the tyranny of a single irresponsible ruler, or chaos and dissolution.

These are the lessons of history, and we shall do well to ponder them, for they are the only lamps by which we may guide our course into that future which inexorably awaits us.

Now we have come to a time when we must recognize that our world has grown so small that it has become, in the sense of this argument, a single community, which can no longer prosper unless its peace can be preserved and the lawless minority among its inhabitants restrained. This is a statement which need not be argued; no exposition of which the English language is capable could be a thousandth part as eloquent as the lessons of the present war and its immediate predecessor. War can no longer be confined within set limits. Its engines are too terrible, its consequences too swiftly felt in every part of our interconnected and interdependent world. It strikes at all, directly or indirectly. A war-mad nation is therefore the enemy of all, just as a criminal gang in a city is the enemy of every inhabitant thereof, and not only of those whom it selects for its immediate victims.

War of today is well called total war.

It is total because its weapons are so complex and expensive as to demand the entire effort of a nation in order to satisfy the demands of a great war machine. It is total because its weapons are such that they strike, not only at the armed forces of warring nations, but at the civil populations, the industrial centers, the whole national territory and everything that lives within it.

As long as the renewal of total war is probable, or even reasonably possible, no nation can afford to be caught unprepared; and preparation for total war absorbs all, or nearly all, the national energies. As long as the renewal of total war is probable, or even reasonably possible, therefore, no other preparation or plan can make much headway, whether in the industrial, the social or the educational field.

This is because, under the threat of war, the future loses its meaning and its hope.

You hope to get a better job after the war? Then you must think in terms of a world in which good jobs will be available. That means that men and women who are in business, or own stock in business enterprises, or have money to invest in such enterprises, can see some good reason why they should stay in business, or get into business, or expand existing businesses—and can place some reliance in the future.

You hope to get married and raise a family? Why? So that your boys will reach military age just about in time to get into the next war? And your girls into munitions factories—which won't be out of reach of enemy bombs the next time? Or so that they may grow up in a world where young people can hope to make something of themselves—amidst all the expanding wonders that mankind has at command in the immediate future if there can only be the opportunity for their development?

You're a farmer, and want to go on farming? You'll need to be able to sell the products of your toil at a fair price, year after year—and that won't happen unless there are those who can buy at a fair price year after year.

You're a young person wanting a better education to fit you for your chosen career? Then you'll want the great educational institutions of this country to pursue their free search for knowledge and truth, instead of being turned into training schools for officers and specialists of the armed forces. You'll want them to have the incentive to go forward that the true teacher, the born educator derives only from the knowledge that he is building men and women who will go out into the world to accomplish better and finer things—not to be slaughtered on the battlefield or spattered in obscene butchery among the ruins of some bomb-wrecked factory.

You're a woman? Then you have husband, sweetheart, brother, son or—dreams of the son you hope to bear. To you these form a more potent appeal than any I could put in words.

You think the government will solve your problems for you? Government is what you make it; it is composed of American men and women like yourself, who are in a sense your servants, and neither better nor worse than you who put them in office. Those men and women can no more make plans for the future than men and women in business, or on the farms, or in the colleges, unless they can see a little way ahead—and they can't do that unless they know that their plans are not going to be interrupted by war. Nor, finally, can those whom you elect to office to administer your affairs adopt *any* consistent policy unless they know that you—all of you, or most of you—will support that policy.

Whoever and whatever you are, you not only have a direct and vital stake in peace, it is the cornerstone of your future. Until that cornerstone is well and truly laid, you have no future worth speaking of or looking forward to.

Peace is your first order of business.

Why yours? Because you're an American, and you and your fellow-Americans control the foreign policy of this country. If you want a foreign policy that will mean a peaceful world, at least for a long time to come, you can have it. But you can't have it just by hoping for it, or thinking it ought to come about. You've got to want it badly enough to see to it that your elected representatives in Congress, and in the White House, want it too; and you've got to keep on wanting it and holding those elected representatives to the mark.

It will cost you something. It will cost our country something. It is too precious a possession to be had cheaply. But it will not cost as much as another war, and unless the cost of peace is paid now and every day from now on, the cost of war will have to be paid again within the lifetime of many now fighting in this one, and at the expense of the children now toddling about our playgrounds.

And what is the price of peace? It is the same as the price of liberty—eternal vigilance.

What we mean by peace, in this context, is the prevention of another total and global war within our lifetimes and the lifetimes of our children. Beyond that we cannot plan; we can but lay foundations upon which those who come after us may build securely.

That we may do this, the first requisite, and the greatest, is faith: faith in our ability to banish the dark shadow of war from our world, and the fear of war from our hearts: faith in the intelligence of the American people and of their Allies to find a way: faith that they will be steadfast in that way, when they have found it.

We must believe that we can have a peaceful world, before we can begin to have it. The greatest enemy of peace is the dark thought which dwells in so many minds, is spread across so many printed pages—"It cannot be done. It never has been done. It cannot be done now."

It can be done. It has been done, and can be done again.

In 1814, there came to an end a cycle of wars which had torn Europe for the better part of two centuries. During that time there had been many political changes, but very little social change so far as the actual conditions of life were concerned. An inhabitant of London, or Paris, or Milan, of the year 1614 would not have been wholly at a loss in the same city in the year 1814. It is true that mankind stood on the threshold of great events. The steam engine was to bring about the industrial revolution; it was just the beginning. Franklin's experiments with electricity had taken place, and many another; but not yet had electricity been put to the uses which it was to serve. New discoveries in medicine were to revolutionize the ancient art of Aesculapius, but these benefits had not yet been conferred upon the human race. Great opportunities were opening wide—but they had been delayed and stifled by the brutal hand of war.

In the year 1814, the Congress of Vienna established peace in Europe following the defeat of Napoleon and the dissolution of his "new order." It was a peace which appeared to be based on political reaction and the principle of legitimism. Actually, it was based on the twin pillars of force and enlightened self-interest, as the event proved. For the peace lasted—lasted long after the forces of political reaction had been disastrously defeated, long after the principle of legitimism was beginning to decay. This peace, the Pax Britannica, which endured for just a century, had been in large part won by British arms, and was in large part shaped by British diplomacy. It owed its long life to the fact that by an accident of geography, the people of Great Britain were so located and armed as to be able to maintain a central position in the European balance, secure from direct invasion in their island citadel, controlling by means of their sea power the avenues of trade which swiftly became so all important to Europe's growing industry, and impelled by the strongest urges of self interest to maintain peace because British trade could flourish and grow only in a peaceful world. For the next one hundred years, British diplomacy backed by British sea power and by the swift growth of financial and commercial power which that sea power made possible, preserved a sort of uneasy, but effective peace in Europe. There were wars, but they were wars of limited extent and duration; they did not spread.

The Pax Britannica was not a perfect peace system, but it worked. It continued to work until the conditions under which it was maintained, that is, the application of British force underlying British diplomacy, and holding a central and impartial place in the European balance of power, ceased to exist; until British sea power was challenged by the growth of the German fleet, and British insular security was subsequently challenged by the growth of German air power; and until the appearance on the world stage of two non-European great powers, the United States and Japan, altered the balance of the world in military and naval strength.

Note carefully that it was force which maintained this peace. It was the equilibrium of land force as between the Continental powers, and the overwhelming sea force of Britain applied impartially against disturbers of the peace, so that there was little to gain by war and no hope of vast conquest. The diplomacy of Melbourne and Palmerston and Disraeli and Salisbury rested squarely upon this secure foundation of force.

In their policy during this century, the British people and the governments which their suffrages put in power were guided, of course, by self-interest—but it was enlightened self-interest. They knew what they needed, and they found a way to get it. And take note of the immense benefits thereby conferred upon mankind. Consider the progress in every field of human endeavor which those hundred years of peace brought forth. Consider the bewilderment of your inhabitant of London or Paris or Milan in 1814, if he were suddenly translated to those cities as they were in 1914. With all the growth of knowledge, of science, of accomplishment, men began throwing off the chains of ancient laws and outworn dynasties. In 1914, every nation in Europe, except Russia, had some form of parliamentary, responsible government. Many were imperfect, but they were there—and even in Russia, the germs of freedom were alive.

Men talked even of a United States of Europe, of a reign of peace under law as between nations. But there were the forces of reaction always steadily at work. There were those who would turn back the clock of human progress. There were those who saw in the approach of a reign of law, the disappearance of their last chance to conquer and despoil others. They struck, while yet there was time, while yet the nations were divided, while yet there was no organized means of restraining them save by each intended victim defending himself as best he might. By tremendous effort, and at grievous cost, they were defeated; but even then the peoples of the free, peace-inclined, law-abiding nations had not learned their lesson. Like the Vigilance Committees of our old West, they dissolved their partnership when the immediate task at hand was done, the outlaws killed or dispersed. So other outlaws arose, took courage, armed themselves, broke the law a few times with impunity, wiped out a few minor members of the law-abiding community and got away with it—and then the whole bitter bloody job had to be done over again.

It is our task to see that these mistakes are not repeated; that the enemies of freedom and peace—and they exist in every land—have no such chance again, in our time or within the future as far as it lies in our power to control it.

Admitting that enlightened selfishness guided the British to the accomplishment of their ends, it was a selfishness not unmixed with idealism. Now, with this past experience to guide us, with the stern lessons of two terrible world wars to spur us on, we find our own enlightened selfishness marching hand in hand with an idealism strongly rooted in our hearts.

Here are, at any rate, the ingredients of success, if we can but mix them in just proportion.

The task which lies before us is, of course, quite different in detail, and much greater in scope, than that which the British accomplished during the century of the Pax Britannica.

The task of preserving the peace of the world after the present war is won will be a far greater task than it was when the dangers to world peace were confined to the nations of Europe. It will be too great a task for any one Power. It will be a task which will require the close cooperation of several powers, and the tie that binds them can be, at least at first, only that of a common interest, a common need for peace transcending every other national ambition.

The problem is different in detail—though not in principle. Though its solution lies in the application of force to restrain peace-breakers, the means of doing so have gravely altered these past few years, and the area within which the restraining force must be ever ready for use has enormously widened; because it is far more difficult to insure the prompt and sufficient application of force, as against a lawless nation, when that force has its origins not within the territory and authority of a single Power, but must be contributed to by several. It is indeed on this last rock that the League of Nations was shipwrecked, and it is the principal threat to every hope we now entertain of finding a solution to the problem of peace.

Yet though modern science has made the engines of war far more formidable than ever before in speed and range and destructive power, this fact—which makes total war so terrible—may do something also to contribute to the cause of peace, if it is properly understood and applied.

It seems likely that a practical solution of this crucial difficulty—as to how a coalition to preserve peace can organize and operate its element of force, its police power—must be found before any such coalition can command sufficient confidence amongst its member peoples to endure for any length of time beyond the hour of victory.

It is to this phase of the problem, therefore, that our practical idealism must first address itself.

3. THE METHODS OF WORLD POLICE

THE PRESERVATION of domestic peace by the use of force has generally been based, not alone on superiority of armament in the hands of the enforcement agencies, but on superior organization and superior numbers, backed by all the authority of public opinion and support.

It is, for example, quite possible for a criminal to acquire an automatic pistol just as good as that possessed by any policeman. It is quite possible for him to outshoot and even kill a policeman. But when he does so, he draws upon himself the full power of the whole police organization, to track him, find him, arrest him and deliver him over to the processes of justice. The criminal may have associates, he may be a member of a gang. But the strength of organized society, and its agency of police, is stronger, commands far greater resources, and has at its service a far more widespread organization than any criminal gang can possibly hope to command.

Most normal human beings know that crime does not pay. Morals aside, most of us know we can't get away with it.

And this is the greatest and most powerful of all the restraints upon lawlessness, the principal bulwark with which organized society protects its members from their own baser natures—the knowledge that crime does not pay, and the knowledge on the part of the vast majority of civilized folk that it is better so. That is why the majority creates and supports the police.

That, also, is why the rise of any criminal organization is regarded as a menace by all good citizens. The stronger the criminals become, the greater the opposing force which they attract to themselves, the greater the pressure of public opinion on its officials to do something effective about the danger. In order to prevent the acquisition of too much power by any individual criminal, or any gang, society passes stringent laws regarding the possession of certain types of firearms adapted to lawless uses, notably such as can be concealed on the person, and such as are capable of a fire-power by which one man can resist several—such as machine-guns. The mere fact that any private individual, or group of private individuals, was known to be accumulating weapons and ammunition without any lawful reason would immediately draw the attentions of the police.

When we come to consider the use of force in preserving the peace of the world community, however, we find certain complexities which must be taken into account. We are no longer dealing with a community composed of individuals, who can be dealt with as such if they break the law, who can be directly taxed to support the peace-enforcement agency, and who can in turn hold it responsible for proper performance of duty, through an established machinery of government. We are dealing rather with an alliance or association of sovereign states, which are united only by self interest and must create, by trial and error and with very little experience to go upon, such political and military agencies as they may require to insure the carrying out of their common purposes.

The great force of public opinion, which is so invaluable a support to the police of lesser communities, must in this case react indirectly, through the media of several governments, and in varying degree according to the feelings and prejudices of peoples of different origins and different points of view. In time, there may grow up among all these folk that unquestioning acceptance of the rule of law which makes the task of law-enforcement agencies so much simpler. But that sort of common public opinion is still to be created; it springs from a confidence which must be earned, which must depend on a record of accomplishment and cannot be created by argument, however cogent.

There is also a basic difference in the matter of armament; and this difference lies at the very root of the problem. Just as a weak and drug-sodden crook with a revolver can kill a strong healthy man who is unarmed, so a criminal nation, given time to acquire modern armament, can overcome a free nation which is unprepared. The disparity between the armed and the unarmed nation is, in fact, much greater than with individuals. We have just seen an unforgettable example of it, in the assault of armed Germany upon her unready neighbors, taking each in succession while the others were unable to do anything to stop her. But the crucial difference between national and individual armaments is the time element.

The individual criminal can purchase or steal a weapon and is at once armed and ready for depredation. The criminal nation cannot arm itself in that summary fashion. It must build up its armaments over a period of years, because to arm a nation for modern war is a matter of: (1) creating a vast munitions industry; (2) acquiring sources of raw materials or accumulating them in enormous quantities from foreign sources; (3) training officers and men to use the weapons thus produced; and meantime (4) assuring the organization, under dictatorial command, of every resource of the state, human and material, for the single purpose of making war.

These are the essential prerequisites of a career of crime in the international field today. They cannot be accomplished quickly, and they cannot be accomplished unnoted. The criminal's purpose must become apparent to his intended victims long before he is in any position to carry it out. Of course, the purposes of the Axis nations were apparent long before they were strong enough to begin the carrying out of those purposes by actual violence. But their intended victims, though these together comprised the vast majority of the inhabitants of our world community, had no common agency by which to deal with a common danger. In none of the threatened countries was public opinion prepared to react with vigor and determination against a criminal assault on some other country as being a peril to itself, much less as being a violation of an accepted and thoroughly understood law, established for the good and sufficient reason that such a law is essential to the survival, the prosperity and the human rights of mankind.

Had there existed such a community spirit and organization, and such a law, or accepted precept, backed by the full force of public opinion in the British Commonwealth, the United States, the Soviet Union, China, France, and the other states now at war with the Axis, the material force available would have been ample to restrain violators of the law at the time when the violations first took place, or the intent to violate it became apparent. Thus in 1931, had Japan, at her first assault on China, been instantly confronted by the threat of drastic and forcible action by all the powers above mentioned, can anyone suppose that the Japanese government would have dared to proceed? Or that any militaristic Japanese government could long have continued in power? Had Germany been so confronted at the moment the first German soldier set foot in the Rhineland, would Hitler have ever been able to bathe Europe in blood?

We may thank a merciful Providence that as weapons have grown in power, so also has grown the time it takes to prepare them. That very power of modern armaments, carrying with it a mechanical complexity and a scale of effort which has never been previously known, may prove in the end to be a blessing in disguise. Not only does it demand of us, imperatively, that we shall find a means to restrain the irresponsible use of such armaments, but also it promises by its very nature that we shall have fair warning of any intention so to use them.

To break the peace, a lawless state must arm itself. Conversely, to preserve the peace, the armament of such a nation must be prevented. To prevent it without a costly war, the preventive action must be taken at the very outset. To carry this process one step farther, it must be apparent beforehand to all concerned that prevention will not only be effective, but that the preventive means will be instantly and vigorously applied if the process of armament for aggression begins—so that it may not even be attempted.

The British during the Pax Britannica did not attempt to prevent other powers from arming; they simply saw to it that their sea power, on which they chiefly depended, was kept at a higher level of strength than the sea power of any prospective opponent or combination of opponents. They were able to do this without undue expenditure of resources and effort, because all their prospective opponents had to maintain large armies and could not compete in the naval field as well. The force behind the Pax Britannica was therefore a special kind of force, sea power, which the British possessed in overwhelming strength and in which they had no serious rival.

The British could always afford to keep a safe margin of naval strength, because they needed no army save a small force of professional soldiers for colonial police work and for the garrisoning of their outlying naval bases.

While these conditions endured, there was never a moment when Britain, if challenged, could not have severed the sea communications of any Continental power, destroyed its overseas trade, cut off and taken its colonies and meanwhile commenced the training of a British army of invasion—which, when the weakened power was fully engaged with its Continental enemies, would have descended on its coast at a well selected moment, on the time-honored plan which had enabled the British to bring to ruin the conquering ambitions of Louis XIV and of Napoleon.

With these examples in mind, none of the other Powers cared to challenge the British, and the British policy of preventing the domination of the continent by any single power, and limiting the spread of any war, was enabled to prevail because the right kind of force was available and sufficient to support it. Only when the new Germany arose, cast aside the wisdom of Bismarck and the lessons of history, and challenged British sea power, did the long peace come to an end.

New conditions bring with them new problems. The British met theirs as the conditions of their day demanded. Today, we must be concerned with preventing the domination, not merely of Europe, but of the world by any single power, and beyond that, with preventing any nation which may have ambitions in that direction from getting hold of the means to carry them out. This is because the weapons of modern war are so terrible in their effect, and strike so quickly, that once the means of aggression are possessed the blows that follow may be overwhelming at the very outset.

This seems to predicate a division of the world into good nations and bad nations; nations which may possess armaments and those which may not. Actually, this is not as silly as it sounds. Every community has certain individuals within it who, on their records, are known to be a menace to their neighbors, and are either shut up in jail or when at liberty are carefully watched by the police. In many communities, the mere fact that a person with a criminal record is found in possession of a weapon is legal cause for his arrest and punishment.

A great many words have been wasted in attempting to find legalistic formulae by which "aggression" may be defined—but in practice, there should be little difficulty in determining the source from which any aggression is to be feared. It would have required neither legal formulae nor profound knowledge of world affairs to have foretold, let us say in 1935, the sources from which the world was in danger of being plunged into conflict. Any reasonably bright ten-year-old child in either Britain or the United States could have pointed out the "bad nations" of that era without the smallest difficulty. So it seems likely to be in the period after this war is won. The governments and the peoples of the nations which are resolved to maintain the peace will rarely be in doubt as to what, if any, nations are a potential threat to that peace.

Therefore their problem will be to see to it that no such potential threat becomes actual.

We have seen that the British, to meet their particular type of problem, used a special kind of force of which they had a virtual monopoly—sea power. At the close of this war, the United Nations, the victors and the inheritors of the responsibility for maintaining the peace they have fought for and won, will be in possession of a type of force which is well adapted, indeed ideally adapted, for preserving the peace, and of which they will then have a virtual monopoly—a kind of force which we may call air power plus sea power.

We must understand what we mean by these terms.

Air power, in the proper sense of the word, is that use of war aviation which strikes directly at the sources of enemy fighting strength, at his industrial centers, rail communications, seaports, and the like. Airplanes used to assist armies are weapons of land power.

Sea power is the control of maritime communications: that is, the use of the sea as a highway for the transportation either of goods or of military forces. Its importance is based on the fact that ships still offer the cheapest and most capacious means of moving either goods in bulk or troops in large numbers, over long distances. It makes no difference by what means these maritime movements are controlled—whether by warships on the surface of the sea, or submarines beneath that surface, or airplanes flying above that surface, or, as is generally the case nowadays, a combination of all three in proper proportion. Whatever the means, if the control of maritime communications is the object in view, we are dealing with sea power.

In maintaining the peace of the world, sea power can function in two ways: (1) by blockade, close or distant—that is, by denying a would-be criminal state the raw materials and foodstuffs which it desires to import by sea; (2) by transporting air power to bases from which the facilities and installations of the law-breaker can be destroyed by the direct action of bombardment aviation.

For the most part, the use of troops need be only incidental in the discharge of these functions. Small, highly trained units of ground troops can be transported by air to disturbed areas, if required, and may sometimes be the best means of restoring order. Small units of specialist troops can likewise be sent by air to carry out, or to complete, the destruction of illegal facilities; these units may operate under the protection of the air forces. Occupation of strategic areas or positions might become necessary. Naval and air bases must be garrisoned against raids, if in proximity to possible sources of danger.

But all of this is based on one essential condition—that the force available is used promptly, as soon as danger is perceived, and before that danger has had time to grow to unmanageable proportions. Specifically, for example, it may be decreed that Germany, a nation with a bad record, shall not be allowed to possess an aviation industry of any shape or character whatsoever. Let us suppose it is discovered that, in a remote corner of Germany, a small engineering works is turning out a few so-called "sport planes." In the tradition of 1919-1939, the result would be a protest to Berlin, a long reply full of weasel words, perhaps an outright denial; months would be consumed in negotiating back and forth, by which time political changes might have taken place in some of the protesting powers and others might have decided that they couldn't risk "going to war" about such a trivial matter. The Germans, meanwhile, finding they could get away with one infraction of international law, would start more plane factories. After awhile, they would be so strong in the air that they could resist any attempt to disarm them by force; and the greater the cost and risk of disarming them, the more the others would shrink from making the attempt. Finally we would be right back to 1938 and 1939. That is the old way, the war way. The police way is different.

Under police procedure, the moment the illegal manufacture of "sport planes" is discovered, the German government is notified that it is breaking the law, that it is required to dismantle the plant under the supervision of police inspectors, and to hand over the persons in charge, including the key technicians, into protective custody for such further proceedings as may seem necessary. If this is not complied with inside of twenty-four hours, the German government is made responsible for clearing all civilians away from the neighborhood of the plant, for at the end of that time it will be bombed out of existence. That is punctually done, and if anybody gets killed in the process the responsibility is squarely on the government of the law-breaking state. And nobody in any of the states which furnish the police aviation thinks twice about the matter, except as an exciting topic of discussion over the breakfast table along with the National League pennant race and the latest Hollywood scandal. It never occurs to any American, for example, to say that the United States is "going to war with Germany" because an American bombing squadron, forming part of an international police force, has in the execution of its duty, wiped out an illegal German plane factory. Everybody recognizes that what the United States is doing, is furnishing its proper quota of a force whose precise reason for being is to prevent the United States from ever having to go to war with Germany or anybody else, by preventing those who would make wars if they could from acquiring the means to do it.

In fact, such a procedure would even deprive them of the incentive. After one or two lessons of this sort, the examples would have their effect; on the same principle that causes crime rates to go down in communities where the police are on the job.

The great thing is that the vast majority of the people of this world, who want peace, shall not again stand by in idleness and hesitation and watch built up, under their very eyes, the machinery by which their destruction or enslavement may be achieved. We did that in the cases of Germany, Italy and Japan during the past decade or two, and now we are paying for a folly over which the historians of the future will shake their heads in incredulous wonder.

The virtue of air power as a weapon of world police is that it can strike quickly, within a period measured not in months or weeks or even in days, but in hours. It can not only destroy by bombing, it can—where such measures are needed—carry troops to disturbed localities. It can "demonstrate," merely by flying over a trouble center, thus perhaps checking trouble by its mere appearance and the terror of its name, now firmly imprinted on human hearts and minds the world over. It can choose its targets, by modern methods of precision bombing, leaving untouched all save the particular object of its righteous wrath. And defense against it is impossible, save by such complicated and expensive devices as fighter planes or antiaircraft artillery, which require a whole war industry to produce in sufficient numbers, and hordes of highly trained men to operate. Proper police procedure would not let a suspected law-breaker get that far.

The principal limitation of air power, as a police instrument, is that of radius of action. That limitation is being reduced by engineering progress, may be reduced still further. But air power in the hands of those who also command the sea can be taken anywhere it is needed. It can operate from prepared and defended bases, supplied both by sea and by air, and these bases need neither be numerous nor heavily stocked with planes; always provided, on sound police lines, that the action taken is timely and that vigilance is never relaxed.

The special conditions pertaining to the operation of air power and sea power from insular bases should be kept in mind. North America is an insular base as regards Europe and Asia; and of course the British Isles and Australia are likewise insular bases. In none of these cases does the base itself require the protection of any large ground force, as long as the air and sea power operating from the base is sufficient not only to guard the approaches, but to prevent the accumulation of hostile fighting power in dangerous strength on a confronting shore. Air or sea power operating from a continental base against an adjacent land power will have to work in conjunction with strong ground forces. The perfect equilibrium of power, and the one to which the natural conditions are best adapted, is a combination of air and sea power operating from insular bases in alliance with land power operating from a continental base. It is this combination, as between Britain and the United States on one hand, and Russia on the other, that is crushing the life out of Germany in this war. That same combination, plus the continental power of China in Asia, should be invincible in the days to come as against any conceivable threat.

But we speak here of the basic conditions of power. For the majority of cases of minor, embryonic threats to peace, for mobility and quick results, air power plus sea power is the ideal instrument for world police action. One more attribute of sea power, already referred to, is its ability to blockade an offending nation. Bombing may not always be necessary; blockade may often be more effective, as preventing the carrying out of aggressive plans by cutting off the supplies necessary for them. But sea blockade alone may not be sufficient; the interruption of land routes may also be necessary. Air power can help to do this, and by its presence and readiness may also help to convince small nations commanding such routes that they need not hesitate to give full cooperation to the police agencies.

Enough has been said to make it clear that the weapons for a good efficient job of world police are available and adequate to such a purpose; and that the maintenance of peace need not be a crushing military burden on the law-abiding nations of the world, nor anything like the burden which would be necessary in reverting to the old conditions.

But, as has been said, no single nation can do this job of world police alone. So, having seen that the means are at hand, and the technical difficulties can be overcome, we must still solve the problem of how a group of sovereign powers can cooperate in the use of those means for such a purpose. However well armed and ready the police force may be, it must act under authority and competent political direction. The very idea of the use of force for the maintenance of peace as among nations, implies not only an armed agency for the application of such force, but also a political agency by which the armament is controlled, and which is properly and legally responsible to the peoples who have created it, and who have made the rules and set the limitations by which its actions are to be governed.

Such a political agency can only function if it has the full support and confidence of the peoples who set it up, so that it may be possessed of the authority to act, under the laws which govern it, without the need for seeking special authorization for everything it does. It can only have such confidence if, in establishing it, it is surrounded with all the jealous safeguards with which free peoples have learned, by bitter experience, to surround those into whose hands they entrust the keeping of their peace.

The growth of national constitutions has shown that, even within single national communities, it is not easy to reconcile the need for giving adequate power to the executive with the need for safeguarding the popular liberties. Systems of government along these lines have usually been slow growths, developing over a period of years and even generations.

As long as the principle of sovereignty continues to exist and to command the primary loyalty of most of the world's people—and we shall not see any fundamental change in that respect in the foreseeable future—it will be a difficult matter indeed for sovereign states to pool, so to speak, any part of their sovereign rights and independence for any common purpose, because the people of each will feel that their nation is becoming just one member of an association controlled by "foreigners." Nevertheless, nations do pool their sovereignties when they form alliances in time of war. In the past, they have done this under the pressure of necessity only, and the alliances have tended to break up under centrifugal pressures as soon as the outside pressure was removed, or sufficiently lessened. Thus the political arrangements of alliances have always been improvisations and have never deserved to be called political systems.

Now we Americans are a member of a great alliance at war. We are assured of victory in that war. Our great purpose is to preserve the fruits of that victory by establishing and maintaining peace. We can do this only by the use of force in proper measure, and we cannot do it alone. Is not the primary solution of our problem to be sought in the preservation of the existing alliance after the war is over? Is not this, perhaps, the first experimental step that we should take on the road which may lead us, slowly perhaps, step by step, but steadily onward toward that "parliament of man" which in some future age may realize those ideals of universal human brotherhood for which we can hardly hope?

4. THE GREATEST EXPERIMENT IN HISTORY

UPON EXAMINATION, it appears that the case for basing the peace-preserving organization of the world on the existing alliance, the United Nations, is overwhelming.

First, the alliance already exists, and its members have, to a greater or lesser degree, had experience in working with each other, and will have more before the war is won. Out of this experience a certain amount of mutual confidence has been bred. The people of each nation are beginning to think of the peoples of the others as friends, to admire their achievements in war, and to be grateful for their contributions to the defeat of those foes who are the foes of all. The members of the great coalition are beginning to act on converging, rather than on parallel lines.

Second, due to the close cooperation which the war demands, there have been, in every echelon of political and military authority, many close personal relationships established which are, and will continue to be, of immense value in promoting international cooperation after the war.

Third, the alliance, at the end of the war, will have ready in its hands instruments and agencies of common effort, both political and military, which can be transformed into instruments and agencies for the carrying out of postwar aims.

Fourth, the people of each of the principal members of the alliance will have fresh in their minds a terrible lesson, learned at bitter cost, that it does not pay to allow world criminals to make preparation for their crimes unchecked; and most of those folk are quite intelligent enough to know that they themselves are in large part to blame for letting such a thing happen a second time, after the previous lesson of 1914-1918.

Fifth, the very name of the alliance—United Nations—will be crowned with victory and has already, even in the mere hope of victory, acquired a prestige and attracted to itself a growing loyalty which is full of promise for the future.

But perhaps the greatest advantage of using the United Nations as the basis for a post-war peace organization is that it already exists—it is a going concern, now in operation. It is hardly necessary to point out how important this is. To wait for victory before planning for the peace is to await the inevitable reaction that may make it impossible to hold the alliance together. Tortured human hearts will yearn for a return to normal ways of living, weary minds may refuse to face responsibilities or to believe that perils can exist greater than those which have just been overcome, and there will also be a perfectly normal and almost irresistible demand to rest and relax after the toil and pain of battle.

Then, as the nations separate, the quick upspringing of little jealousies and little greeds, growing to noxious strength under the whiplash of demagogues—divisions, quarrels, confusions, compromises and "adjustments"—and we have once more the world of international anarchy in which might makes right and in which Napoleons and Hitlers are bred.

Hitler and his Italian and Japanese accomplices are criminals, but they have done us one service which we should never allow to be undone for the benefit of future Hitlers: they have united all the peoples of the world whose future welfare is dependent on the maintenance of peace. It was the menace of the Danes which forced England to become a united nation. It was the menace of a British tyrant which forced the thirteen colonies to unite and form this American Republic. These unities were maintained, became permanent, to the great benefit of the peoples concerned. This new unity, the United Nations, if we make it live, will confer even greater benefits on all the peoples of the world.

We have already noted that one of the greatest obstacles to the creation of a permanent organization to maintain world peace is lack of faith—faith in our ability to carry out so great and so unprecedented an undertaking. No less an obstacle is the lack of faith among our people that the others have the same objective, the same necessities as we, are equally concerned to keep the peace, and will loyally do their share. We have, as a nation, a congenital fear that we are about to be outsmarted; that something is going to be put over on us. There are still those among us who are violently opposed to any sort of international cooperation, and it is upon this fear, this distrust, that they harp most strongly.

Now a certain amount of healthy skepticism as to other people's motives and intentions is a good thing. Our whole constitutional system of checks and balances is based on the sound belief that it is better not to trust human nature too far, that such important matters as the rights and liberties of the people need to be carefuly safeguarded even against the people's own elected officers. Certainly, in so important a matter as the national safety, there should be no question of blind trust of other nations. America must always, facing the uncertainties of the future, be prepared to take her own part, to uphold her rights and her honor. A weak and unready America can have little influence as a member of the family of nations.

Nor need we suppose that other great Powers will place any childlike confidence in us, or commit their fortunes to our keeping. They won't, nor have we any right to expect that they will.

We are, however, now associated with other nations—quite a number of them—in the abatement of a danger common to all.

We are fighting this war, not alone, and not just for our own selfish aims, but as a member of a great coalition, for the ultimate aim of establishing a peace from which all the members of that coalition, indeed all humanity, will benefit.

The cement which binds the coalition together is a common interest—victory over the common foe. Then is it not possible that these powers should continue to work together, when victory is won, to assure themselves of its fruits? For all of the major Allies, those fruits are chiefly to be found in the maintenance of peace. Neither Great Britain, nor any of the British Dominions, nor China, nor the United States covets the territory of any of its neighbors. It is claimed—without much proof—that Russia does, but the charge usually goes no farther than the Baltic States, the Polish Ukraine and Bessarabia. This means a buffer area, a strategic frontier. Obviously, the more confidence the Russians have in any joint system of security, the less will be the need for a strategic frontier which will involve very serious internal problems of police and administration.

The Rusians are genuinely interested in the maintenance of peace. They need peace probably worse than any other of the United Nations—China possibly excepted.

But old prejudices, on both sides of the Russian border, die hard. Probably there is no more important single achievement in our march toward unity and a controlled peace, than the bringing about of closer relations, a greater degree of mutual confidence, between Russia and the two western Allies, Britain and America. Both political and military considerations must be taken into account in moving toward this goal. Not until we have the Russians sitting with us, and with the British, in close and frank consultation, can we say that unity is a fact among the majority of the peoples of the world—that law-abiding majority which must in the future take upon itself the task of keeping the peace. The Moscow and Teheran conferences are, for that reason above all others, great and notable achievements.

As to our three major Allies, the first task after the war will be the urgent problem of national reconstruction. Of getting people back to work; of building up the industrial plants, the homes, the transportation systems, the whole vast fabric of national life that war has broken. Of wiping out the black traces of the enemy's devastation. Of starting afresh to live and build and pursue happiness.

In a measure these will be our American problems too. The people of all these lands, and ours, will be vitally and urgently interested in these things, and these things can be had by them, and by us, only if we are to have a world free of war and fear of war in which to accomplish them.

Therefore the tie of self interest will still bind us together. We will still have a common purpose, a common enemy. We will still have something to do, something which we shall all need to do, which no one of us can do alone, but which we can do by a common effort. Within those limits we may therefore have confidence in each other—as long as the common purpose continues to be common. It is not a question of what Mr. Churchill desires, or Marshal Stalin, or the Chinese Generalissimo. It is a question of a need which cannot be denied, which the people of all these lands feel, and see, and believe in, and are determined to have, once they can be convinced that it is possible, and that the only way it can be attained is through united action by all of us—and that everyone concerned will "play the game."

That is why our own American responsibility is so heavy. Nothing will go so far to convince the British, the Russians and the Chinese as action by the people of this country—definite action—which commits us to do our part in preserving the peace of the world after victory in this war has been attained, and demonstrates that we intend to tackle the problem on practical and earthy lines, step by step, with firmness of purpose and with faith in our ability to succeed. Only so shall we be able to command both the respect and the confidence of others.

It is necessary at the beginning to be both realistic and cautious. It is idle to suppose that any arrangement which is wholly satisfactory to every participating nation will be reached at the outset. There will have to be compromise, a whole series of compromises. There will have to be strict definitions and limitations. There will have to be adequate provision for future change, just as there is provision for amending the Constitution of the United States, which is also a series of compromises—albeit an unusually successful one.

But if realism warns us against expecting to have our own way altogether, caution likewise warns us against trying to prepare detailed blueprints in advance. It is no more possible for Americans, or Britons, or Russians, or Chinese now, in the midst of this war, to sit down and write out the future fundamental laws of mankind, than it would have been possible for the signers of the Declaration of Independence, in the midst of war, to have foretold in 1776 the exact terms of the Constitution to which many of them would set their hands in 1787.

Moreover, it would be rash to go into great detail now, because of the opportunities thus afforded to those who, in all our United Nations, are opposed to any sort of international agreement for collective security. Whether such opposition arises from a blind and selfish nationalism, or from even less creditable motives, it is present and it is a force to be reckoned with.

One of the most attractive methods open to that sort of opposition is the attack in detail upon any proposition which may be made looking to international cooperation. It was thus that the United States was kept out of the League of Nations by the isolationists of that day; not by a frontal attack on the whole basic idea of the League. Such an attack would have failed. But by whittling down the extent of our participation by a reservation here and a reservation there, what remained was left without meaning or value. The same tactics would be used today against any detailed proposition which might be put forward; but these tactics lose their effectiveness against a step-by-step development of the existing alliance, the United Nations, which is now engaged in the winning of this war and which, as it proceeds with that great task, may also develop within itself the mechanisms and the spirit which will enable it to win the peace. To make a blueprint of the future now would therefore be not only futile, but dangerous to all our hopes, just as would have been the case had the Constitution as finally adopted been published to the nation along with the Declaration of Independence.

The Constitution was created by men who were great enough to understand that the vital thing was that there should be a Constitution, embodying fundamental principles on which there was general agreement, even though it is probable that no single delegate to the Convention was wholly satisfied with every Article and clause of the Constitution as finally adopted.

Our new structure must likewise be created, in the first instance, by men who are great enough to see that the vital thing is that there shall be an international organization strong enough, sufficiently well-knit and stable, to put an end to total war and give civilization a breathing space; even though none of the participating nations may be altogether satisfied with every detail of the plan which is finally adopted. Also, its creators must be men who are great enough to have the patience and the wisdom to see that so fundamental a change in national relationships can only come as a natural growth, not as the sudden imposition of a new and startling reorganization of this ancient world.

There should, then, be little talk now of a world government, a world parliament, a super-state. That may come, but it is unlikely to come in our time. It will be difficult enough to accustom people to the idea of giving up even that modicum of national sovereignty which is necessary in order that there may be a central authority with power to keep the peace. Realism will tell us that the force behind any such authority, based on the conditions of the coming victory, must be force supplied by the four major United Nations—the British Commonwealth, the Soviet Union, China and our own United States. But to state this baldly arouses at once all sorts of anxieties among lesser nations, and angry accusations from the idealists, that these four powers are proposing to "run the world." Hence the need for a crystal-clear understanding of just what we *are* trying to do. We should seek to achieve no more than a central authority of carefully limited, defined and safe-guarded powers to do certain specific things relating to the maintenance of peace, the restoration of order in disturbed areas after the war, the supervision of the disarmament of enemy powers, the administration of international relief and perhaps of temporary governments in areas where no local government exists or can immediately be created.

In our hearts, all of us are probably ready to accept, and take for our very own, the central idea and ideal of a just and lasting peace among all peoples. We may not be ready to accept any particular detailed scheme for attaining it; but we are ready to accept the thing itself, just as the people of the thirteen Colonies were ready to accept the Declaration of Independence. The essential step to be taken now is not the making of the detailed plan, but the general acceptance of the principles which the final plan, whatever it may be, must embody and support. The idea and ideal of United Nations must take tangible form now, in the midst of war, just as the idea and ideal of United States took tangible form in 1776, in the midst of war. Then we too shall have our bright banner, and we too shall follow it to victory over our enemies, and to the reaping of the fruits of victory as well.

The form which that victory will take, the time it will take to win it, the cost of it in lives and suffering and treasure, are all dependent in very large measure on the extent to which this central idea and ideal take hold upon the hopes and imaginations of the men and women of the United Nations now, as the war moves from the stage of defense and preparation to the offensive and decisive stage in which the initiative is ours.

This is so, because a defensive war may be fought with no other political objective than simple self-preservation; but offensive war invariably has, or acquires, other political objectives. These may be related, or seem to be related, to the idea of self-preservation, as in the matter of so-called strategic frontiers; or they may come to be of quite a different character. From this tendency, in a war of coalition such as the present, there emanate a thousand evil genii of suspicion and ill-will; for the people, and even the statesmen and soldiers of each and every member of the coalition, begin to suspect that they are fighting in some degree for the actual or suspected political objectives of the other members, which may not be compatible with those of their own country. When the natural growth of these suspicions is accentuated by the clever and persistent propaganda of a desperate enemy who well knows that the success of that propaganda is the last slender hope of his escaping even in part the consequences of his crimes, the situation is even more dangerous.

The first task of the architects of peace is therefore clearly defined. It is the presentation of peace to the peoples of the United Nations as the one great political objective of the war, an objective great enough to encompass all or most of the particular national political objectives, an objective which the peoples can understand, accept and make their own, and in which each of them is vitally concerned, a practical objective which can be attained by understandable, definite means. When that is accomplished, then and only then is true unity of purpose and action to be achieved in an offensive war by our great alliance. The actual attainment of the objective is a political accomplishment; it is not to be attained by military victory—victory merely makes it possible. It is essential that our central political objective shall be simply stated, in broad general outline, in principle, so that it can be understood by all; it is a banner, not a book.

To repeat: The central political objective of this war must be a just and lasting peace throughout the world.

On that objective there can be complete unity of heart and mind among all the peoples of all the United Nations. Only if the security of each, the peace of each, becomes the responsibility of all, and only if the assumption of that responsibility by all the others be confidently believed in by the people of each nation concerned, can there be to any degree an abandonment of purely national objectives, a pooling of national interests for the common good. Only if a tangible beginning is made now, only if the bright banner is actually lifted to the sun for all to see, borne forward by the hands of all, can there begin the growth of that mutual confidence which must be the cornerstone of all our hopes.

The whole conduct of the war from now on, in its military as well as its political aspects—the disposition of forces, the choice of directions and times of attack on the enemy, the very means by which the war is waged, the attitude of states now neutral, the moral and psychological factors both on our side and in the enemy's camp—will be influenced more or less by what action we of the United Nations now, as our offensives are launched against the foe, may take to give assurance to each other, to the enemy and to the world at large, as to the permanence of our union and the uses to which we mean to put the victory which will presently be ours.

To be more precise: What is now required is the formation of a United Nations Council, representing all the United Nations, whose first task should be the formulation and issuance to the world of a simple, clear, understandable statement that we are fighting to establish a just and permanent peace, and that to attain that object each nation pledges itself to remain united with the others after victory is won; that each stands ready to make the necessary sacrifices of its own particular ambitions, as far as may be necessary, while giving solemn assurance that it will assume its fair share of the necessary responsibilities. This statement should, in definite terms, recognize the fact that the maintenance of peace in any community must be based on the controlled and intelligent use of force, under proper safeguards, in the hands of a law-abiding majority.

The meetings of the heads of government of the four major Allied Powers at Cairo and Teheran, and especially the statement issued after the Teheran conference, are steps in the right direction. But they are temporary steps, of which the effect will pass unless it is reinforced and made permanent by the establishment of a continuing agency for inter-allied cooperation. Logically, a United Nations Council should be the next step, in order that all the good results of Cairo and Teheran may be conserved.

The organization and functioning of such a Council will, of course, be in large part dependent on the attitudes taken toward it by the governments and peoples of the states participating in it. To a great extent it will have to make its own way; it will have to win confidence in order to possess it. The nature of the problems with which it will have to deal will depend on the course which the war takes. For example, had such a Council existed at the time it might have done much to prepare in a political sense for the invasion of French North Africa and later of Italy. Therefore, our consideration of the reaping of the fruits of victory must concern itself with an examination of the probable course of the war, of the political and military problems which will have to be dealt with during its progress, and of the means which may be available or can be created to deal with them, as well as of the conditions which will or may exist when hostilities come to an end in Europe and in Asia—events which will probably not be simultaneous. Much of this must be surmise and conjecture; but of this central fact we may be sure:—

Into the hands of the victors in this war, the fact of victory will deliver over, for good or ill, the dominion of the world for the time being. Upon the use which we of the United Nations, as victors, shall make of this hour of triumph, the future of our civilization assuredly depends. The least we can do is to begin now, not to make detailed plans for that future, but to create the atmosphere of confidence in which such plans can thrive when at last they come to be made. To that end, the creation of a United Nations Council is the first essential step. It will be the beginning of the greatest experiment in history, an experiment upon whose outcome depends nothing less than the preservation or destruction of the human race.

5. A UNITED NATIONS COUNCIL

WE, THE PEOPLES of the United Nations, need to start thinking and planning now as to how we are to reap the fruits of victory. We need to talk these vital matters over among ourselves now, because we are on the offensive, and therefore we are now going to be confronted almost daily with the need for making political decisions of great importance. Either we will come to an agreement in advance as to general policies, or decisions will be taken by generals on the spot, or by statesmen in their several capitals, which will not command the adherence of all of us—and then there will be trouble.

The dangers of a new war, after this is won, can be quite accurately defined. When this war is over, the United Nations will possess all the fighting power there is in the world, save for a few weak and scattered neutrals. The enemy states will be defeated and disarmed.

Therefore, the dangers of a new war will lie in one of these three possible categories:

(1) The enemy states, or one or more of them, may be permitted to recover, rearm and start a new war.

(2) An entirely new threat may arise from some source not now apparent.

(3) We of the United Nations may fall out among ourselves.

None of these things can happen if the United Nations remain united, and firm in our purpose to maintain peace. Our unity is our guarantee of freedom and happiness.

That is why it is so vitally important that we should anticipate any possible threat to that unity; that we should take every possible measure to preserve and guard it.

We must be united as to our policy toward the enemy states, and as to the security measures to be taken to prevent a resurgence of trouble from those quarters.

We must be united as to our policy in matters of relief and reconstruction, so that normal conditions of life may be restored as rapidly as possible in as large an area of the world as possible.

We must be united as to our policy in matters of armament, and its use in preventing any threat to peace from any new quarters.

If we remain so united, we need not fear that civil strife, ideological or otherwise, will threaten our peace from within, for peoples weary of war and scarred by its fires will turn readily away from it to the building of their futures and the pursuit of happiness—once they see the unity assured that shall guard them against war and shall lift from their spirits the fear of war.

Divide, said the Roman tyrant, and rule. So also reasoned Hitler. Against the forces of division, the weapon of the people is unity. Against the threat of war, the policy of the free nations must be unity. Never before in the history of the world may it be so truly said, by so many peoples in so many lands, united we stand, divided we fall.

But we must begin now, because the dangers of division are already arising, with the problems that the approach to victory, the first successes, have already brought and will bring in increasing measure from this time onward. As these words are written, the problems of France, Poland and Italy are all tormenting the chancelleries of the United Nations, and those of the Balkans may have to be taken in hand before this book is in print. And then there are the problems of East Asia just around the corner.

What, for example, is going to be the future of Poland? What territory will be included in the new Poland? Will it have the seacoast of East Prussia, or another corridor? Will it have its old eastern boundary, or a new one more satisfactory to the Soviet Union?

Are we to give recognition to the French Committee of National Liberation as a provisional French government? If not, by what authority will that Committee rule in French metropolitan territory when and if French liberation is secured in whole or in part? Or will some new United Nations authority be set up there? Or will we just drift, and find ourselves confronted by some distasteful *fait accompli*—or by chaos and civil strife?

What is to be the future of the Netherlands Indies? Of French Indo-China? Or Burma? Are we to set the old rulers back in power? Are we to promise the peoples of these lands anything better than a return of the old system, or better than the junior partnership in the "East Asia Co-Prosperity Sphere" which the Japanese are now engaged, not without some success, in selling to them? If so, what?

One could go on and on. Obviously, all too obviously, we have not in these matters attained any degree of political unity. That is not because there is no desire for unity, though it may be because the approach of victory has to some extent blinded the unthinking as to its necessity. But in large part, the lack of unity is because there is no machinery for assuring it, not even a common meeting place where these vital questions may be currently discussed.

In military cooperation, we do much better. The case of Italy will serve admirably to illustrate how well we do in the one, how poorly in the other—and to point the moral that what the soldiers can do, the statesmen can do also if they will.

The fall of Mussolini and the sudden taking over of power by the King and Marshal Badoglio found the two Powers actually engaged in attacking Italy—Britain and the United States—without a political policy adequate to deal with the situation. As a result, the American propaganda agency said that the fall of Mussolini was unimportant, and later made a personal attack on the King and Badoglio, which the President had to repudiate; while the liberal press sputtered and fumed over treating with Badoglio at all, and the British Foreign Minister told the House of Commons that Britain would treat with any non-Fascist government which would surrender unconditionally. In the end, the whole matter was passed to the Allied commander in chief, General Eisenhower, because he *did* represent a joint Anglo-American authority in the military field, whereas there was no such joint authority in the political field save by way of the occasional personal conferences of Mr. Roosevelt and Mr. Churchill. But the French are also vitally interested in the future of Italy, and so are the Yugoslavs and the Greeks, and so—as far as Italy's future affects that of the Balkans—are the Russians. Not until the conference of Moscow was a United Nations policy about Italy finally agreed upon.

Now what is clear here is that the political policy of the United Nations has not been as well coordinated as the military policy. It is possible that a great opportunity was lost in consequence. General Eisenhower has done a magnificent job of coordinating British, French and American armed forces in the Mediterranean. He drove the Axis forces out of Tunisia, and then launched so violent a blow at Italy that he toppled Mussolini from his place of power and knocked the last vestige of the will to continue the war out of the Italian people. He thus prepared the way for a political *coup de main* which might have had much greater results than have in fact been attained, for the Germans were far from ready, at the moment, to deal with the sudden change in the Italian situation by force. But political hesitance and unpreparedness missed, at least in great part, this opportunity. The Germans, recovering swiftly from the shock of surprise, as they always do, acted with their customary energy to restore the situation, and now our troops are fighting a hard battle to conquer the Italian peninsula from the German armies.

There will be many explanations of this, especially when the war is over, but I venture to say that at the bottom of it all lay a failure on the part of American and British political leaders, especially diplomatic leaders, to realize that the key piece, on that particular chessboard at that moment of opportunity, was not the King of Italy, nor yet Marshal Badoglio, nor even Eisenhower's military successes. The key piece was the war-weary, disillusioned people of Italy. They were the ones who wanted to get out of the war, and quickly. The United Nations wanted them out, and wanted to gain possession of their territory before the Germans could move in. The military arrangements by which the United Nations brought the Italians to this state of mind were perfectly designed and executed. The political arrangements which were essential in order to cash in on the military success were either nonexistent or defective.

The reason the military arrangements were so good is because there exists, in Washington, an organization called the Combined Chiefs of Staff, where British and American military policy is carefully worked out and coordinated by competent officers of both nations. Under the direction of this organization an Anglo-American Commander in Chief, in the person of General Eisenhower, was appointed to command all the armed forces of both nations, and as it has turned out, those of France also, in the western Mediterranean. General Eisenhower proved unusually well adapted for this task, and created a staff in which British and American officers worked side by side—were, indeed, almost interchangeable. The results of this admirable policy, and its admirable execution by General Eisenhower, we have already seen in Tunisia, in Sicily, and in Italy itself.

For the political arrangements of the United Nations, there exists no such coordinating agency, no such trained and competent staff. There have been consultations, yes. But consultations by telephone between capitals thousands of miles apart, or occasional personal meetings of leaders, are very different from a permanent *organization*, where men work together day by day in the making of plans, the solution of difficulties, the attainment of acceptable compromises and the formulation and support of general policies.

I have given so much space to this matter of Italy because it so perfectly illustrates the point at issue.

The United Nations are, to some degree at any rate, making their military policy a joint policy. They are not going much beyond that. They have not yet created an agency to fix and crystallize and then seek to achieve the political objective of the war.

There are signs, hopeful signs, that some progress is at last being made in this direction. The Moscow, Cairo and Teheran conferences helped immensely, and their great success, the upsurge of hope which followed, is clear evidence of what might be achieved by a more permanent agency of union. The creation of the European Advisory Council in London, with representatives of Britain, the United States and Russia, is a step forward. So is the new Mediterranean Council, in which those three powers plus France, Yugoslavia and Greece are represented. Perhaps the true United Nations Council with a global rather than a sectional view, and with the ability to plan a total policy for a total war, may come from the pooling of the activities of these groups with the rather tentative and uncertain work of the Pacific War Council at Washington. However it may come about—and experience warns us that such growths are usually the result of trial and error plus the urgent pressure of necessity—we need a real United Nations Council very badly; I had almost said desperately.

To try to run the affairs of this great coalition without it, despite military efficiency, is like trying to run a great manufacturing business with a first rate production staff but no board of directors.

We need the Combined Chiefs of Staff—perhaps with more nations represented eventually than, as at present, just Britain and the United States. But we need political unity as well as military.

How should such a United Nations Council be composed, and how shall it do its work?

Shall it be composed of heads of states, heads of governments? If so, it will include President Roosevelt, Prime Minister Churchill, Marshal Stalin, Generalissimo Chiang Kai Shek, and the chief executives of the other United Nations. Of course, all these men cannot, for obvious reasons, sit down together every day to plan the war. But the work to be done by the United Nations Council is of such paramount importance that it ought not to be intrusted to persons of less responsibility, that is, political responsibility, than these men who stand at the heads of their respective nations. No other voices can speak with so much authority; no other decisions will be so readily accepted as being responsibly authoritative, both by their own peoples and by others.

The great difficulty is that all of these men have important tasks to perform, as heads of governments, which they cannot neglect, and which require their physical presence at their respective capitals most of the time. Those capitals are far apart. Even though the airplane has made a thousand miles a matter of three hours, instead of the three days of our fathers, or the three weeks of our grandfathers, considerations of time, of politics and of security will not permit constant travel back and forth by these eminent personages while war still plagues the world and its circumambient atmosphere.

Therefore, whichever capital of the four chief United Nations may be selected as the seat of the Council, three of its leading members will be perennial absentees. A possible solution—and it is not a wholly satisfactory solution, but a compromise between what is desirable and what is attainable—might be a system by which these heads of states would be the actual members of the Council, but would be represented by deputies save on occasions of great importance.

The distinction between a Council composed of heads of

states, who are actually and physically represented by deputies most of the time, and one in which the said deputies might appear as members in their own right, is one which must be very carefully examined. It must be considered in the light of the constitutional relationships which the chief executives of the several Powers bear to their legislative bodies and to their people. These relations differ. There is no substantial difference, for example, between Mr. Anthony Eden, sitting at the Council's table as a representative of His Majesty's Government in the United Kingdom, and Mr. Anthony Eden in the additional quality of a personal representative of the Prime Minister. Not only is Mr. Eden's own personal prestige very considerable, but under the British system, the official acts and utterances of one member of the Cabinet involve the responsibility of the Cabinet as a whole. And since he would not be there at all unless the Prime Minister chose him for the task, his authority and prestige would be little different as Mr. Churchill's deputy than as a representative of the British Government in his own right.

With Marshal Stalin and Generalissimo Chiang Kai Shek the case is quite different. These two men are not constitutional leaders in the sense in which Mr. Churchill is a constitutional leader. They are not liable to be dismissed from office by an adverse vote of a legislature.

They are, for the present at any rate, supreme in their own lands; in their own persons they embody the supreme political and military authority of their respective countries. Theirs and theirs alone is the power to make the final and binding decisions. Therefore, in the United Nations Council, it will be of the utmost importance that these personal leaders shall be represented by deputies, personal representatives, who have their full confidence and who can be intrusted with a considerable latitude in making decisions; men who know the minds of their chiefs on matters of broad general principle, and can be trusted to take care of the details themselves. Admittedly it might be difficult to find such men. Admittedly, and especially in the beginning, there might be a good deal of referring to headquarters for instructions. But it does seem vital that, as to Russia and China at least, the men who represent them at the Council shall be the personal deputies of Stalin and Chiang Kai Shek.

Finally, we may consider the position of the representative of the United States. We have here no such system of collective Cabinet responsibility as exists in Britain and the British Dominions. Our representative ought certainly to be the personal deputy of the President, who is constitutionally charged with the conduct of our foreign relations. But there is an added consideration, which applies to no other country, but of which every other country is acutely aware in its dealings with the United States. The President does not have the final voice in our foreign relations. He can, as to any treaty he may make, be overruled by the Senate; in fact, by one Senator more than one-third of the Senate; worse, by thirty-three Senators representing seventeen States containing only eight per cent of the population of the country. This is a defect in our system of conducting foreign relations in these times, whatever may have been its virtues in the early days of our Republic. It is a positive danger to our hopes for peace, for those hopes must be built on confidence, our confidence in others, and theirs in us. They ought to be able to know that our word is good when given, and not subject to subsequent repudiation under conditions in which domestic politics and personal bias may play a destructive part.

The Connally resolution is a step toward establishing such confidence, but hardly enough in itself. Another such step would be for the President to invite the Chairman, and perhaps one or two other members of the Foreign Relations Committee of the Senate, to participate in future important United Nations conferences. A Constitutional amendment abolishing the procedure by which treaties must be ratified by a two-thirds vote of the Senate, and substituting therefor ratification by a simple majority of both Houses, would be a third useful step forward.

But even these will not be enough. We need a practical device by which we can ensure the collaboration of the executive and legislative branches of the government in the formulation of foreign policy. The plan suggested by Mr. Nathaniel Peffer in the August 1943 issue of *Harper's Magazine* seems as good as any that could be devised. Mr. Peffer proposes that there should be a standing committee, meeting regularly to discuss the foreign affairs of the United States, to consist of the President, the Secretary of State, the Secretary of War, the Secretary of the Navy, the Chairman and ranking minority member of the Senate's Committee on Foreign Relations, and the Chairman and ranking minority member of the Committee on Foreign Affairs of the House of Representatives. This plan would not only serve to keep Congress informed, it would also imbue the legislative branch with a measure of responsibility for formulating policy. It would be very difficult for Congress to reject a treaty which had been concluded as a result of policy so determined. Moreover, the degree of confidence which other nations would have in the commitments which the President might make would be enormously increased. The conduct of our foreign relations would then be brought into balance with the needs of the times, and without doing violence to our constitutional system of separated powers. But it would be essential in adopting such a plan that due publicity be given to the new arrangement, in order that it be known by all; and that the new standing committee should have a permanent, and if possible a legal status, with an established secretariat and offices. Only by so doing can the necessary confidence and understanding be gained. The informal and occasional conferences so dear to the heart of our present Chief Executive simply will not meet this need.

If all this were done, the representative of the United States on a United Nations Council could sit as the deputy of the President, and in some degree also as the deputy of the Congress.

I have gone thus at length into the qualifications of the representatives of the four major United Nations, because it is essential that we clearly understand just what is proposed, and also the very considerable complexity of the problem—and of all problems attending cooperative agencies formed, not by individuals, but by sovereign states possessing very different political institutions.

Other nations will have their own questions to solve in choosing their representatives. But the important thing is that there shall be a Council of the United Nations, that it shall be composed of persons of as high a degree of responsibility as possible, and that it shall begin to function as soon as possible. The way to begin is to begin. Other bridges can be crossed as we come to them.

It should not, however, be expected of the Council that at first it shall make momentous decisions every day. One of its main functions should be that of a discussion group—a place and an opportunity to talk things over, where everyone's views can be heard and where differences, which seem formidable in the cold language of diplomatic notes, can be discussed, reduced and perhaps even eliminated. The pooling of political information would alone be of immense value.

Nothing is more common, as any reporter with Washington experience is aware, than to have some highly placed and responsible official say: "I'd tell you more about this if I could, but frankly I just don't know what the facts are"—or, "I don't know what lies behind the Russian (or Chinese, or Spanish or what not) position in this matter,"—or, "We did receive an answer to our note, but we couldn't understand what they were getting at, and we're asking our Embassy to try to clear it up. One thing's plain, there's been a misunderstanding somewhere along the line." If the United Nations Council can do no more than to pass around the table *all* the information on a given subject, so that everyone can have a clear look at the facts; if it can do no more than make everyone's position, and the reasons for it, clear to everyone else; if it can do no more than eliminate some of the misunderstandings which are inevitable in the conduct of international affairs at long range, it will have more than justified its creation.

Naturally, there will be something more to such a Council than just a big room with a table in it and a chair at the table for each member. The Council must have a permanent secretariat to carry on its business, circulate its memoranda and keep its affairs in order. Each nation represented will wish to provide its representative with a staff, probably including military, political and economic advisers. Various members of these staffs will form subcommittees, some of which will be permanent, and some transitory in nature, to deal with particular phases of the Council's work.

The Council will, of course, keep in close touch with the military situation, in order that political difficulties affecting that situation may be anticipated if possible, and political advantage taken of opportunities created by military success. However, there should not, for the present, be any question of the Council taking over the supervision of military operations, though it might be of help in matters of coordination.

Its influence and authority will have to grow with practice, and it will be important not to attempt too much at first. As its members and their staffs become accustomed to working together, the scope of their activities will grow.

Much will depend on the degree of confidence and the measure of authority given by the respective heads of states to the deputies whose task it is to represent them around the Council's board. This will of course vary, by reason of the personalities involved, and by reason of the constitutional differences as to the authority of—for example—Mr. Roosevelt as contrasted with that of Marshal Stalin. Here again, time will tell. The more useful the Council proves, the harder will the participating states and their leaders try to improve it and the more authority and freedom of action they will grant their deputies, as necessity appears.

As a beginning—as has already been said—the Council should be charged with the task of setting forth, in simple clear words, the political objective of the United Nations in waging and winning this war. The peoples of the world should be rallied to the cause of peace, and the general principles behind the methods which it is proposed to use to preserve the peace should be stated—not in great detail, but in broad principle.

This charter of peace should serve the United Nations much as the Declaration of Independence served the United States. It will be an announcement of a sacred purpose, to which the peoples of the world are invited to pledge their allegiance. Every effort should be made to obtain ratification of the peace charter by the proper constitutional authority in every participating nation at the earliest possible date.

That will be the beginning. Thereafter the Council can begin to function, can organize its machinery and settle its procedures, and go to work. There will be enough and more than enough to do.

From every point of view, it is to be hoped that the first session of the Council, that at which the Peace Charter is adopted and promulgated to the world, may be attended by all the heads of states who are the proper members of the Council. This would be especially important, not only in dramatizing the vital importance of the Council, and of the unity among the nations—of which unity the Council is at once the symbol and the instrument—but also in assuring the Council and the charter, from the very first, the greatest possible degree of public confidence.

There are one or two special problems to be considered in connection with the formation of the Council. The first is, that Russia is not at war with Japan and so far—save at the Moscow and Teheran conferences—has held aloof from any open participation in United Nations military and other planning groups which must, of necessity, consider measures against Japan as well as against Germany. Of course the Russians are quite right, both from their point of view and from ours, in avoiding as far as they can the necessity for dissipating their strength in a two-front war. It is to everyone's present interest (the Axis excepted) to have Russia able to concentrate her efforts against Germany, without suffering the drain of another war, in Asia, several thousand miles away. But actually this Russian caution is in large part a matter of keeping up appearances. No one, certainly no Russian with any knowledge of world affairs, supposes for a moment that Japan is influenced, one way or the other, by any considerations of international law or morality, as far as the question of Japan attacking Russia in Eastern Siberia is concerned. The Japanese will do that, or refrain from doing it, strictly as they see their own interests in the matter. If they think those interests will be served by such an attack, they will make it at their chosen moment regardless of the most scrupulously correct conduct on the part of the Russians. Indeed, they will select their moment with the idea of catching the Russians off guard; they will probably choose a time when they are ostensibly doing their best to improve Russo-Japanese relations. The great risk which the Russians would run in joining, for example, the Combined Chiefs of Staff, would be that the Japanese might thereby become convinced that the Russians intended to attack them, either at once, or when the German danger has been liquidated; at present, Tokyo may be nursing some doubts on that point. Certainly it might cause the Japanese, in desperation, to attack first on the theory that their chances would be better if they struck while the Russians were still fighting Germany. But this situation is obviously eased by every day that the downfall of Germany comes nearer, and it is likewise eased by the blows which are being struck at Japan in the Pacific and elsewhere, blows which are slowly eating away the air power, the naval power and the shipping of the Nipponese Empire. The time is not far distant, certainly, when the Russians can feel free to accept, if they will, an invitation to join a United Nations Council or any other interallied agency without any anxiety as to what the Japanese may do. And, that very practical consideration aside, the advantages of direct participation in the remaking of the world in general and of East Asia in particular will surely appeal to so clear-thinking and far-sighted a man as Marshal Stalin.

The second special problem is the question of the smaller Powers. One of the principal objections which has been voiced to the creation of a United Nations Council is that with some thirty nations participating, it would be impossible to reach concrete and practical decesions without endless debate and emasculating compromise. This objection has much force in the matter of military decisions, because of the time element, but it is not proposed to turn over the control of military operations to the Council. These operations are being carried on, almost altogether, by the four great powers, Britain, Russia, China and the United States. As China is not now in a position to take offensive action, it may fairly be said that there are only two centers of paramount military authority—the Anglo-American Combined Chiefs of Staff at Washington and London, and the Russian High Command at Moscow. As long as these two achieve a reasonable degree of coordination, and there is much concrete evidence that they do, the purely military direction of the war is being conducted as efficiently as can be expected.

As for political questions, it seems unreasonable to assert that thirty national representatives cannot come to any agreement just because of their number. In many of the problems to be discussed, a good number of the participants will have no direct interest and may thus act to some extent as arbiters. Moreover, no question should be brought before a plenary session of the Council until it has been thoroughly examined, threshed out and reduced to its essentials by subcommittees composed of the Council's expert advisers. Finally, we must recognize as a matter of course that the influence of the great Powers will usually be decisive in the end, so that where these four (or perhaps five, with the rebirth of a free France) are agreed, the others will fall in line. That does not mean that the lesser Powers will be subject to the tyranny of the greater. The forces of public opinion in such countries as Britain and the United States can be counted on to take a liberal and just attitude in most cases, and to support a little nation in proper demands. But it does mean that disputes cannot be dragged out to unreasonable lengths, and it does mean that the great central objective of world peace cannot be permitted to come into danger by reason of the inability of two small nations to come to a fair settlement of a minor dispute.

We must recognize, and frankly accept, the fact that there is no such thing, under modern conditions, as a small state which is of military account, or which can do anything very much to sway the course of a great war one way or the other—except by giving passage to, or affording base facilities for the armed forces of a great power. If the peace of the world is to be preserved by force, that force will, in the immediate future at any rate, be provided by the four powers which form the backbone of the United Nations. They cannot be hampered in their application of that force by any nonsense about the neutrality of small nations. The small nations whose security is preserved by that force must give every facility for its prompt and effective exercise, just as a good citizen must take a policeman in his car to pursue a fleeing criminal, even though he runs some risk thereby. The citizen cannot declare himself neutral because in all that he does he is accepting the benefits of police protection, a protection which he can never provide for himself. The small state of the post-war period will face precisely similar circumstances. No small state can possess the vast industrial machine and the resources necessary to wage total war. Lacking them, it is at the mercy of the armed criminal power unless it is protected by the police. Hence it must help the police, on demand, in the only way it can. This should be clearly understood by all concerned. It is one of the new facts of life, whether everybody likes it or not.

Another objection which has been offered to the creation of a United Nations Council now, while the war is still in progress, is that this is no time to get into an argument over these thorny political questions. But this is surely an objection which must be examined in the light of the alternative, which is inevitably that each power will make its own decisions as it goes along, will indeed be compelled to do so in its own interests. These decisions may well be at variance as between the several powers concerned. The results of such a process can only be a series of unilateral commitments, of mortgages on the future, which will surely be far more dangerous to unity, to cooperative effort, and even to the conduct of the war, than will the full and even brutally frank discussion of these problems by the means, and under the conditions which a United Nations Council would make possible.

Take the exceedingly troublesome question of the eastern frontier of Poland. It has got to be settled sooner or later. Is it better to postpone examination of it, meanwhile pretending to ourselves that it doesn't exist, and so leave it to be settled, in all probability, unilaterally by the Russians, by force of arms? Or is it better for the Russians and the Poles to talk it over, in a special subcommittee of a United Nations Council, with the British and ourselves sitting in as friendly arbiters, and to examine it not by itself, but in relation to all the other phases of the Polish territorial problem—sea coast, frontier with Germany, frontiers with Czechoslovakia and other countries, and the future of Lithuania? Note how this problem bears on the whole vitally important question of better and closer relations between Russia and the western Allies. The Russians have long cherished the suspicion that Britain and the United States, or at least some influential persons in those countries who might some day come into political authority, want to create what is called a *cordon sanitaire*, of which a strong Poland would be the keystone, to check the spread of Russian (or as some say, of Communist) influence to the west. Realistically, of course, this is sheer nonsense. There is no way, under the conditions of modern warfare, of making Poland or any of her neighbors strong enough to do anything of the sort if the Russians mean to expand by force. As we have already remarked, there is no such thing as a well-armed small nation. And if the Russians do not mean to expand by force, then the *cordon sanitaire* policy does not make sense. This Polish question is therefore an excellent opportunity, if it can be discussed and settled now, of convincing the Russians that their western allies do view the future realistically and clearly, that we have confidence in Russia's intentions to deal fairly with us and with her neighbors, and that we will deal likewise with Russia. Under such conditions it is hardly to be doubted that the Poles could obtain everything to which they are properly entitled, and that the three great Powers would be able to eliminate a cause of present and future friction between them, to the vast benefit of all concerned.

It is precisely because some statesmen are acting as though it were impossible to settle these matters, as though they were too delicate to be discussed, or even mentioned in any voice above a whisper, that so much future trouble is now being stored up for postwar explosion. It is precisely because this has been our own attitude, that we have run into so much difficulty in French North Africa, and in Italy. It isn't beyond human powers to arrive at a settlement of *any* dispute, if it can be approached in an atmosphere of good will and under conditions which make it difficult for either side to resort to the irresponsible use of force.

One more vitally important need would be filled by the creation of such a United Nations Council. It would be an outward and visible sign of unity between the several nations, the unity on which the peace of the world depends. It will uplift the hopes and bolster the faith of the peoples of those nations. They will see in it the fulfillment of their dreams of peace. They will rally to the standard it raises, and they will see to it that their governments do not betray them. If proof of this assertion is needed, the results of the Moscow conference have recently afforded it.

Without such real and whole-hearted faith on the part of the people of all these lands, there is not much hope of a lasting peace. The concrete fact of the creation of a United Nations Council will do more to win popular confidence than all the words that could be poured out on the subject.

But how will those hopes, that confidence, be fulfilled when Victory is won? What will be the function of the United Nations Council then? What will be the procedures by which peace may be assured?

To answer those questions, we shall have to examine the conditions under which it seems likely that the war may end, and the probable course of the war up to that point; the political as well as the military events which are to be expected, and which will affect those conditions—and we shall have to take into account the fact that it is very likely that the war will end in Europe before it ends in Asia and the Pacific.

6. THE DEFEAT OF GERMANY

THE ACCEPTED STRATEGY of the United Nations, now being carried into effect, is based on the fact that they have two enemies, Germany and Japan, which are widely separated geographically, and which must therefore be attacked separately. Having in mind the factors of time and of preparation in relation to time, the United Nations do not find themselves able to deal decisively with both their enemies at once. They are therefore compelled to choose which they shall destroy first, to concentrate their main effort on that one, and to contain the other in the meantime. The logic of the facts makes Germany the first, and leaves Japan to wait its turn.

The principal factor in this decision is Russia. The largest land force and one of the largest air forces of the United Nations belong to the Soviet Union. Those forces are wholly engaged in fighting Germany, and cannot—while German troops are deep in Russian territory—be transferred elsewhere. The Russian forces are thus fixed, and the movable forces—the air power and the amphibious power of the United States and the British Commonwealth, with the wonderful strategic flexibility which is conferred on those powers by complete command of the sea—must, in accordance with the most elementary principles of warfare, be used to assist the main United Nations effort, the Russian effort. This is the decision that has been put in effect. To have done otherwise would have been to give the Germans a chance to recover from their present injuries and to concentrate against the Russians. This might well have resulted in a separate Russo-German peace, either as a result of German success or of Russian disgust, and then the Germans would have been free to turn all their strength to dealing with Britain and our bases in Africa and Italy while our main forces were out in the Pacific. Moreover, the distances in the Pacific are so great, and the conditions so difficult, that it may be a long time before we can come really to grips with the Japanese. The Germans, on the other hand, are closely beset. Besides their Russian front, they are being directly attacked both from Britain and the Mediterranean. Their major ally, Italy, has been knocked out. Their other allies are of doubtful allegiance. The European neutrals are beginning to turn against them. Their problems become less soluble with every passing day.

And—their industrial power, the source of all their evil strength, is being weakened by air attacks on a scale never before known in the short but lurid history of air warfare.

Therefore, the only conceivable United Nations strategy is to keep on hitting Germany with every available ounce of strength until Germany capitulates, and then to deal in like manner with Japan.

There remains to be considered the question of method. As to that, there are two schools of thought, as far as Anglo-American effort against Germany is concerned. The one believes that we should put all our bets on smashing Germany from the air. The other believes that we cannot defeat Germany by air power alone, and must invade the continent of Europe and defeat the German armies on the land. The extremists of these two schools are very far apart. The more moderate thinkers are quite close together. Most air officers now believe that invasion will be necessary in the end. Most ground officers now recognize that air power can do much to soften the resistance of the enemy, to prepare the way for invasion, and to reduce its cost. The differences, except those of the extremists, are merely differences of degree: how much of our total available resources shall we put into air power now, and at what point shall invasion begin?

There would be no difference at all, in these matters, if it were not for two inescapable facts. The one is that our output of fighting power is not unlimited, but must be divided between the weapons of air power and those of land warfare—the same thing, of course, applying to our resources in fighting men. The second is that—as happened in North Africa, and is happening in Italy, and will happen elsewhere—the application of these tremendous forces brings about changes in the enemy's military and political situation, changes which must be foreseen, and against which the proper preparations must be made in advance.

As far as may be judged by events, the Anglo-American decision for 1943 was to give air power its chance to soften up the Germans, while collecting powerful invasion forces in Britain and North Africa, re-opening the Mediterranean to save shipping, and driving home heavy blows against the outlying allies of Germany, especially Italy. Every support was meanwhile given to the Russians that the capacity of the lines of communication made possible, and everything possible done (1) to weaken the Germans in their fight with the Russians; (2) to divert German forces from the Russian front to other fronts.

All this is almost certainly a preparation for a full-scale invasion of western Europe from the British Isles when the time comes. That time will come when the German reserves have been largely absorbed elsewhere, when German fighting power has been fatally weakened by air attack, and when sufficient Anglo-

American forces are ready for the task. This invasion will be designed to bring about decisive results.

This is making war with the inexorable certainty of mathematical calculation. The Germans can do no more than run around inside their narrowing circle of defenses, patching up a hole here and a hole there and at the same time trying to defend themselves from overhead attack, until at last they are completely overcome. That is the theory, at any rate, upon which we seem to be proceeding; and it is a theory which events, for the most part, tend to justify.

We have still to consider, however, first, just what the Germans can do to defend themselves; and second, the human factors involved, which tend to distort the cold perfection of mathematical formulae.

The leaders of Germany know, of course, that they cannot hope to win. Their sole concern is that they, or their successors of like mind, should have a chance to try again. Nothing will ever induce these men to abandon their innate belief in Germany's God-given right to rule the world. They are thinking wholly in terms of a German comeback—not now, not next year, but sometime later on. Their frame of mind is precisely that of the professional criminal who, after a series of successful robberies, finds himself at last cornered by the police, and whose thoughts at once turn to getting off as lightly as possible, and to the new and bigger and more successful career of crime upon which he intends to embark as soon as he gets out of jail.

These German leaders, whether political or military, know that for the time being, at least, the game is up. They have lost. They are confronted by superior force, and their own force is diminishing. Even the neutrals are turning against them. Their allies are wavering, will soon begin to fall away. Their second attempt to gain the dominion of the world, that "manifest destiny" in which they so firmly believe, has failed.

But let us not suppose for a moment that they have ceased to believe in it, or do not intend to try again.

Their immediate object is to save something, some remnant of power or at least some remnant of prestige with their own people, from the debacle. They have been confronted with a demand for unconditional surrender. If they yielded to that demand at once, not only would they be discredited, but Germany would have such a blood bath as has not been known in that country since the Thirty Years' War. The insulted and injured would have their revenge. In that process, it would be very likely that all the fight would be taken out of those Germans who survive, so that for generations to come German parents would hand down to their children an abiding fear of war and an abiding hatred of those who would lead them to war.

So, from the point of view of the Prussian military caste, the real leaders of Germany, the war must go on, but with an entirely new political objective. Take note that the political objective of any war dictates, inevitably, the character of the war; and in turn, the political objective must be brought within the compass of the military possibilities. There is no use fighting for something you know you have not the power to attain. Germany is now constrained to fight a defensive war. Her political objective, therefore, must be such as a defensive war can secure for her, if it is successful. And as the Germans understand so well how to wage total war, war with every resource and every method coordinated to a common end, we may be certain that it is not only by military, but by every available means that the political objective of Germany will be sought, at every stage of the war.

That political objective will be to save something out of the wreck of German hopes. It will be to make peace on any terms which will leave the present leaders of Germany, or those who think of Germany's future in like terms, with some chance of making a comeback when Germany has recovered her strength and when Germany's enemies have forgotten and relaxed. This war was begun by the Germans in the full conviction that this time they would repeat none of the errors of 1914-1918. The next war will be begun by the Germans, if they get the chance, in the conviction that they can avoid the errors of both the present and the last war; that this time they will get away with it. That is how the criminal mind always works. Otherwise there would never be such a thing as an habitual criminal.

The whole idea of the defensive war is to make the subjection of Germany cost us so dearly that there will come a point at which the United Nations will modify, to a greater or less extent, their demand for unconditional surrender. Anything at all that can be gained is a net gain. Even the gain in surrendering to organized Allied forces at the borders of Germany is a gain over surrendering now and being massacred by the uncontrolled but justified fury of the Poles, Czechs, French and all the other cruelly victimized neighbors of Germany. The material destruction which must come with a prolonged war does not count in such calculations; factories and dockyards and homes can be rebuilt. What counts is the keeping alive of that evil spirit which the German leaders regard as their sacred fire: the spirit that will, they hope, some day enable them or their successors to build up a new legend and set forth once more on a career of conquest.

But a defensive war requires leadership of a different character than that of an expanding war of conquest with a revolutionary drive behind it. It requires, if it is to achieve any degree of success, a cold, calculating military leadership of a very high order of efficiency, and possessing complete authority to act in accordance with the dictates of military necessity. If a province, as Frederick the Great once put it, must be given up in order to save two provinces elsewhere, there must be no hesitation in doing so. Such procedures are difficult for a government whose dynamics are those of the Nazi revolution. Nazi fanaticism has been fed on the legend of its own invincibility. It has no moral resources with which to face defeat. Hence it seems very likely that there may be a shift of power from the Nazi party to the Army.

The ability of the Army's leaders to achieve such a shift would seem to be unquestionable; I use the word "seem" because it may not prove so simple a matter as it appears to be on the surface. It was just this possibility which some of the more sober Nazi leaders foresaw long ago, and which caused some of them to advise Hitler against bringing on a general war. "When Germany goes to war," they warned, "all power goes to the Army. And no one can predict how the Army will use that power in any crisis that may arise; nor can anyone predict the nature of the crises which may arise." Hitler appears to have been confident that he could win the war, and deal with the Army later, when he no longer had need of it. But unfortunately for this calculation, he has lost the war. He is now face to face with the fact that the leaders of the Army may decide that they can achieve their new and necessarily limited objectives better without their Fuehrer and his Nazi associates.

When we speak of the leaders of the Army, we speak of the real rulers of Germany. The Prussian military caste, not all of whose members are soldiers, but all of whom have the same ideas about Germany's "manifest destiny," are the men behind this war. They will also be the men behind the next war, if they are given the opportunity. They will continue to be the men behind the wars until they are destroyed, or until they have conquered the world. They found the Nazis very useful, as being possessed of a leader and a formula which could whip the German people into ranks, inspire them with revolutionary fervor, command from them blind obedience even unto death. But now the Nazis are not only a menace to their military plans, but to the gaining of their present political objective—a negotiated peace. Nobody is going to make peace with the Nazis.

From the Nazi point of view, this situation is likewise only too apparent. The Nazi leaders are interested in one thing mainly—the saving of their personal skins. They have not the smallest interest in seeing a gang of Prussian generals surrendering Germany to the Allies in a polite conference, and thereafter retiring to their country estates to live the lives of landed gentry until better days shall come. They have a pretty clear idea that, in order to make such a thing possible, there will have to be a little purging done first, and they know who is going to be on the receiving end of that purge. In June, 1943, Die Schwarze Korps—organ of the most fanatical of the Nazis—said editorially: "We fight for our naked lives and nothing else." The Nazis need not submit to an Army purge like trapped chickens. They have weapons. They have the Gestapo and the S.S. They may decide to do some purging of their own, and to purge first.

All these are, at least, examples of the human elements that may enter into military plans and upset the nicety of their calculations of power and time and distance.

The harder the blows which we strike at Germany, the more critical these problems become. The greater the tension, the more urgent the need to act for self-preservation. The chances are that, openly or covertly, the Army will take over power, and that Germany will go on fighting a defensive war. But other things may happen, too; and certainly there will be internal strife and dissension, which to a greater or less extent will weaken the German power to resist. It may even bring about a collapse of that power. It would seem almost certain to do so, if it were not for the factor, already referred to, of "the insulted and injured."

That factor has a direct bearing on the will to resist of the

German people, and on their ability to retain that national cohesion which is essential to the power of resistance. In a beleaguered state like Germany, under the conditions of total war, the fighting forces and the civil population are almost indistinguishable. There is no chance of the one holding on if the other weakens. In other words, every German old enough to fight, to work, or to help the war effort in any way, male or female, is a part of the defense of Germany.

Now the fighting spirit of the Germans, as a whole, has rested, from the beginning of this war, on two pillars. These pillars are of unequal strength, and one grows stronger as the other grows weaker. The first pillar is a lively expectation of the fruits of victory—a Germany supreme in a world where the Herrenvolk would be masters and all others inferiors or even slaves. The second pillar is an equally lively appreciation of the consequences of defeat—for eighty million Germans surrounded by something like twice that number of Poles, Czechs, Yugoslavs, Frenchmen, Belgians, Dutchmen, and Norwegians, all with the fires of a German-made hell burning in their tormented hearts.

As long as the Germans were able to think of ultimate victory as certain, and later even as possible, the first pillar was the stronger; as that dream faded, the other pillar became the stronger. Today it stands almost alone, but it is a sturdy growth.

And well it may be. For unless the organized and disciplined fighting forces of the United Nations are able and willing to prevent it, the final collapse of German fighting power—the moment when the Germans cease to be able to supply and munition the Wehrmacht—will see the beginning of a series of massacres such as Europe has not known since the Peace of Westphalia brought the last of the dread wars of religion to an end.

The Germans know this very well. Many of them—perhaps

the majority—are quite convinced that they have the choice between going down fighting, and being slaughtered in some highly unpleasant way by the peoples whose hate they have drawn upon themselves. But many of them hope that if they fight hard enough, they may get terms which will—in the end —save them from either fate.

There is no reason to draw fine distinctions between the German people and their leaders. After all, the Germans are human beings. They have a moral responsibility for what their leaders have done, and what they have helped to do. It is childish to say that we are at war with Hitler only, or with Hitler plus the Prussian militarists only, and not with the German people. We are at war with Germany, and every German is our enemy until he stops fighting and accepts the only terms we have to offer—unconditional surrender. Which is to say, we don't make terms with criminals. They can give themselves up, if they like, and throw themselves on the mercy of the court: the court of outraged humanity. That is the best we can offer. It is the best we have any moral right to offer.

But if that is to be our policy—that is, the American policy —then we should make certain that it is also the policy of our Allies. We know it to be the policy of the British; but is it the policy of the Russians? Of that, there was in the beginning some doubt, in view of Russian official and unofficial statements. The Russians were not to be blamed for making their own policy in the absence of any United Nations policy; but all of the foregoing examination of German conditions cries out the urgent need for having a United Nations policy about Germany, as well as about a great many other matters.

In this direction, there can be no doubt that the Moscow conference of foreign ministers made a great advance. Other and perhaps even greater steps toward unity of policy between Russia and the western Allies were taken at Teheran, where Roosevelt, Churchill and Stalin met. The need for political unity is being recognized under the pressure of events which military unity has brought about. That need will grow by reason of the nature of the events which are to follow.

We should see quite clearly what the effect is going to be of the means which we are using to attack Germany, and the steps the Germans may take to defend themselves.

We are attacking Germany in both of the ways which are open to us—by blockade, and by assault. These are the only ways to attack a country, just as they are the only ways to attack a fortress. They are complementary, and usually necessary to each other. Total war is unlikely to be brought to total victory except by the use of both means, fully employed and wisely coordinated.

Blockade strikes at the enemy's means of making war, seeking to weaken or disarm him. Assault strikes at his armed forces, seeking to overcome them and penetrate into his home territory. Before the invention of the airplane, blockade could be said to be external pressure, while assault sought to exercise internal pressure. This distinction no longer stands, for air power has made it possible to carry on an internal blockade as well as an external one. The operations of long-range air forces are, indeed, a form of blockade rather than a form of assault, curious as this may sound. These operations are directed at industrial facilities, railways, docks, shipping, canal locks, and other fixed targets of like nature. Their purpose is to prevent the enemy from moving raw materials from their sources to manufacturing centers, and from moving finished munitions from manufacturing centers to the fighting fronts. It makes no difference, in principle, at what point this process is interrupted—or how: whether by destroying a railway bridge between the mine and the factory, or destroying the factory itself. The basic idea is to disarm the enemy by depriving him of the means of making things to fight with. The more complex the industrial processes become, the more vulnerable they are to air attack at well-chosen vital points—for example, note the very serious injury done to the whole German war-production by the raid on the Schweinfurth ball-bearing factory. Of course there is a reverse side to the shield: the better equipped a nation becomes, the better it is able to build up defenses against air attack: fighter planes, anti-aircraft artillery, searchlights, listening devices, warning systems, fire-fighting apparatus and all the rest.

But constant readiness for defense against air attack must be maintained at every possible target within reach of enemy bombers. This in sum total amounts to a huge diversion of fighting power: it ties up men, planes, guns, equipment, and it diverts a vast flow of industrial output into a purely static defensive system, which has to be everywhere ready, all the time, but only small parts of which are actually engaged at any one time.

The moral effect of air attacks must also be taken into account, particularly as regards the civilian population. These effects extend not only to those living in bombed areas, but to all those under constant strain and required to take constant precautions, and even to those with whom the refugees and the homeless must of necessity be billeted.

Whether air power by itself can be decisive in a war against such a nation as Germany has been a matter of much controversy. It is a controversy that may never be decided. If the Germans were to offer to surrender unconditionally tomorrow, there would be enthusiasts to claim that air power did it, and there would be counter-enthusiasts to claim that the Russian Army did it. The fact is, of course, that if there were no Russian Army, the Germans would be able to put a lot more effort into defending themselves against Anglo-American air attack, and if there were no air attacks they would be able to do much more against the Russian Army. You can carry this a little farther and point out that if there were no British and American navies, there would be no air attacks, or at least not effective ones, because, though the larger types of planes can be flown across the Atlantic, the smaller types (equally necessary), and the vast supplies of fuel, lubricants, spare parts and supplies which are necessary to keep a great air force in operation could not be brought to British shores because of the U-boats; and likewise, the Russian Army would not be as tough a customer as it is, because it too is getting a great deal of its best equipment from the distant arsenals of North America and Britain. Total war is not to be carried on effectively by one means alone, but by the coordinated use, under intelligent direction, of all available means. It is teamwork that is the key to victory, not any one form of fighting power.

But the effect of these various means must be carefully noted. The naval and land blockade, plus the air attacks, weaken the German ability to produce weapons. Their tendency, as we have said, is to disarm. The Germans are living in the very crater of a human volcano. As long as they can sit on the lid, it will not erupt. The moment they can no longer sit on the lid, the pent-up flames will rise to consume them. That moment is the moment when their armaments for the control of their occupied regions cease to be superior to the means which their captive peoples possess for attacking their conquerors. As the flow of weapons from the German factories diminishes, that flow will more and more be absorbed by the troops on the fighting fronts—the Russian front, the Italian front, the other land fronts which Anglo-American armies may open, and the air defense front. The greater the political power of the Army, the more it will be able to see to it that its demands are met first. But the leaders of the Army are not such fools as to suppose that they can go on holding frontiers which include occupied hostile territory, while allowing the captive populace to get out of hand behind their backs for lack of means to restrain uprisings.

Thus the air attacks on Germany are directly, though only in part, responsible for the necessity under which the Germans find themselves of abandoning some of the more distant of their conquests, of reducing their fronts and shortening their lines of communication, as they are doing in Russia. They will do this according to plan, if they can. They will try to avoid ruinous losses, the cutting off of any great part of their forces as in Stalingrad and Tunisia. They will try to wring from this process every possible ounce of military and political advantage, to gain every possible moment of time, and to leave behind them the greatest possible legacy of troubles great and small for us to have to deal with.

The more of our shipping, our material and our effort we must use in feeding starving populations in territory formerly occupied by, or allied with Germany—the more enemies we make for ourselves in trying to police the chaos the Germans will take care to leave behind them—the more misunderstandings the Germans can conjure up out of these difficulties, in order to represent us in an unfavorable light to those whose opinion is still of value to them—the more half-baked criticism that is launched at the head of this or that Allied statesman or government from within his own land—the more all of this happens, the better off are the Germans. Their military weapons have failed them; their political weapons are their last resort. If above all they can do anything to produce dissension among the major Allies, they may yet be saved. They will leave no stone unturned to accomplish this.

In particular, they will hope to find some way of dividing Russia from the western Allies. Once again, we come to the Russian question—this time, from the military viewpoint.

We have seen that the United Nations are attacking the Germans by blockade, and by assault. In the beginning, Britain and the United States did most of the blockading, and the Russians most of the assaulting. That means that the Russians were losing a hundred lives where we and the British were losing one. There is no use arguing that the Russians had to fight the best way they could when they were invaded, and that the western Allies are now fighting the best way they can. The point is not how the Russians had to fight when they were on the defensive, or how the British had to fight when they were all alone, or what expedients had to be resorted to to keep the Germans in check until the power of America could come across the ocean and find bases for its attack on German-held Europe. What counts now is the very realistic question of how best to defeat the Germans, and how to do it most quickly.

The time factor is of paramount importance. To waste time in war is to waste lives. When you have the initiative, when you are on the offensive, the most humane way to fight a war is to prosecute it with the utmost fury until victory is won; this will always cost less in lives than to drag out the war by half-measures and the hesitating search for the ideal, which always gives the enemy time to build up his defenses and resist you more strongly. In a coalition war such as this one, it is doubly important that time should not be wasted, for time gives the enemy the chance to try to separate the allies by political maneuvers of all sorts. Time allows frictions to arise, and frictions are sure to arise if any one of the allied nations is wasting time, or even seems not to be doing its full share of the fighting. When the sacrifices in lives by one of the Allies are much greater than those of one or more of the others, it is particularly easy for such suspicions to take root, even though they may not be justified. It is in lives that plain folks count the cost of war first and foremost. They are much more impressed by the fact that their John, or their Pierre, or their Ivan isn't coming home any more—or by the total number of Johns or Pierres or Ivans in their home town who aren't coming home any more—than they are by any wordy argument whatsoever, no matter how sound in principle.

Therefore, in considering how Germany can best be further attacked and brought finally to complete defeat, we must take into account the point of view on this subject of our Russian allies.

The major front in Europe has long been the Russo-German front. The Germans are in no doubt about that. They have two-thirds of their army and half their air force tied up there. If that wasn't so—as remarked above—our air attacks and our amphibious operations would not be doing so well. Now, whatever we and the British may do in the west, the Russians in the east are not going to be able to defeat the Germans on that front except by a decision on the ground. If we westerners are going to help such a decision, we have got to do it by weakening the German ability to fight the Russians on the ground.

Air power can do that in two ways—by diverting German fighter aviation, which prevents the Germans from giving the essential degree of direct air support to their armies in Russia, and by smashing the German arsenals so that those armies cannot be supplied with as many weapons. Possibly in time this might be enough. But it is not the quickest way to win the war, for it is neither using all our power, nor is it absorbing the enemy's reserve strength in all categories. In particular, it is not diverting and absorbing the enemy's reserves in that category in which the Russians are most interested: his ground forces.

This is important to the winning of the war, and it is likewise important to that Allied unity which is essential not only to the winning of the war, but to the winning of the peace.

Let us be quite clear about this matter. Underneath many of the arguments that are made for putting all our eggs in the one basket of air power, there is the assertion that by so doing we will save thousands or tens of thousands of American lives, or British lives, or both. But that is true only if it is the quickest way to win the war. The proper criterion is not, can such and such material destruction be effected by airplanes at a less cost in lives than by landing an army and fighting one's way to the stated objective. In many cases, of course, it can. But the real point is: can the war be brought to an end more quickly, under conditions as they now exist and with the means we now possess, or will possess within the next year or so, (and we know quite well what those means are and will be) (1) by concentrating our efforts in western Europe on air attacks; or (2) by combining air attacks with a major invasion of the European continent, which will draw off German troops from the Russian front and compel Germany to fight on two land fronts, as well as to defend her vital centers from air attack?

If the latter method will end the war sooner—materially sooner—than the former, experience tells us that it will be less costly in lives, despite the terrible casualty lists that may seem, for the time being, to belie that assertion. The casualty lists of a great battle are shocking because they occur all at once. American public opinion was profoundly distressed, for example, by our losses at Salerno. The shock would be worse if we lost ten thousand killed in one day in smashing our way ashore on the Belgian coast. The shock would in fact be much greater, and would occasion much more comment, than if we lost fifty thousand men scattered over a period of a year's desultory fighting that need never have taken place at all.

The Russian position is that we have no right to hold back an invasion if we are doing so simply for the purpose of saving lives, and if in so doing we are prolonging the war for them as well as for us. That contention is perfectly fair and just. Probably it is strategically correct as well. And certainly, an Anglo-American invasion of the continent of Europe in great force would be a master stroke in the political sense, because it would do so much to draw the Russians closer to us in every way.

These considerations appear to have resulted in a decision to invade western Europe as soon as possible.

Thus, the Germans face not only intensified air attacks (within the limit of our means to intensify them, as affected by other requirements) but also the prospect of having to fight on two major land fronts, while at the same time keeping in check the civil populations of their conquered territories.

What measures will they take to meet these conditions?

The area which is vital to their defense is considerably less than the area which they now occupy. We must place a reduced value on the question of raw material sources, such as mines and forests and food-producing areas. These were of great importance to Germany in the full tide of her conquering offensive, not only to expand that offensive and make it stronger, but also as taking away the resources with which the victims might defend themselves. But the offensive having failed at last, the Germans have been busy hoarding up reserve stocks, and they will, as they give up territory, sweep the land clean of everything they can use, leaving the wretched people to starve or be fed and maintained from Allied resources. As long as the Germans can hang on to the Lorraine iron mines, the coal and iron of Polish Silesia, the Rumanian and Galician oil fields and the mineral deposits of Yugoslavia, these, with their imports of Swedish iron, their own native resources, and their accumulated reserves, will enable them to carry on a long defensive war—a war, indeed, whose issue will almost certainly be decided on the battlefield before lack of raw materials begins to paralyze the German sword arm.

From the industrial point of view, Germany's resources are also very great. Her industrial district in the Ruhr valley has been the principal target of our air power, and has suffered severely; so also have other western industrial centers. The Germans have tried to counter this loss by transferring industries to safer areas, and by building up the existing industries in other parts of the territory they control—notably, in Czechoslovakia, Austria, and Silesia. They have decentralized their industry as much as possible, especially their aircraft industry. There is, of course, a limit to what can be done in these directions.

The production of steel, for example, is not an economical process except in close proximity to large coal fields. It is not by chance that Pittsburgh, Gary, and Birmingham are great steel centers; it is because the coal is there. The same is true of Essen and Pilsen. It is possible to bring the iron ore to the coal, but it is not possible, under ordinary conditions, to bring the coal to the iron. This is because the bulk of coal in producing a given amount of steel is so great, that long hauls from mine to foundry are not economical.

The Germans are not particularly worried about production costs as far as balance sheet figures are concerned, but they must take into account the terrific strain now being put on their railways and canals. They are short of locomotives, cars, and barges. Their transportation system is one of our major air objectives, and it is suffering from all the ills which beset the German industrial plant as a whole—shortage of labor, of repair facilities, of lubricants, of well nigh everything. The moving of German industries from the places where the natural laws of economics caused them to be originally established, to other sites dictated by strategic necessity, imposes unnatural strains on this harried transportation system, which is yet another reason why the Germans must give up distant conquests in order to be able to carry on at home. But there seems no reason to suppose that the industrial resources of Germany, plus those of western Poland, northern France, Belgium, the Netherlands, Czechoslovakia and Austria, will not be sufficient to enable the Germans to wage their defensive war for a long time to come, provided that the Germans can give these industries a reasonable degree of protection from air attack.

From the strategic point of view, the Germans must take into account first of all the geography of Europe. The most important terrain feature of the European continent is the great mountain wall of the Alps, extended eastward by the Carpathians, which stretches right across the middle of Europe from the Gulf of Lions to the western end of the Black Sea. North of this wall lies the north European coastal plain, which begins at the Pyrenees, includes most of France, all of Belgium and Holland, and almost all of Germany and Poland, sweeping on to the east to lose itself in the vastness of the Russian steppe. The would-be invader of Germany must fight his way into the central portion of that plain in order to reach Germany's vital centers. He must, therefore, have a foothold in France or the Low Countries on the west, or in Poland on the east, or he must land from the sea, or he must storm the passes of the mountain wall on the south.

At this writing, the Anglo-American forces have no foothold in France or the Low Countries. To get one, or to invade Germany from the German coast or through Denmark, they must effect a landing against opposition that will certainly be more powerful, more concentrated and better coordinated than the opposition to our landings in North Africa, Sicily and Italy. The German defensive measures in the west will certainly take into account the fact that such a landing can be made a very costly operation; they will seek to get all the benefit they can from this circumstance, even though they may not intend to make a protracted step by step defense of all the territory behind the landing points. No landing can be made against strong defense except under the most complete air cover, which as a practical matter restricts a landing in western Europe, based on Great Britain, to that part of the coast of Holland, Belgium and France which lies within 100-125 miles of British air bases—this being the practical limit of fighter radius of action, if the fighters are to have sufficient time in their operating area to do a thorough job. Roughly speaking, that means that a large scale invasion of that western shore must come

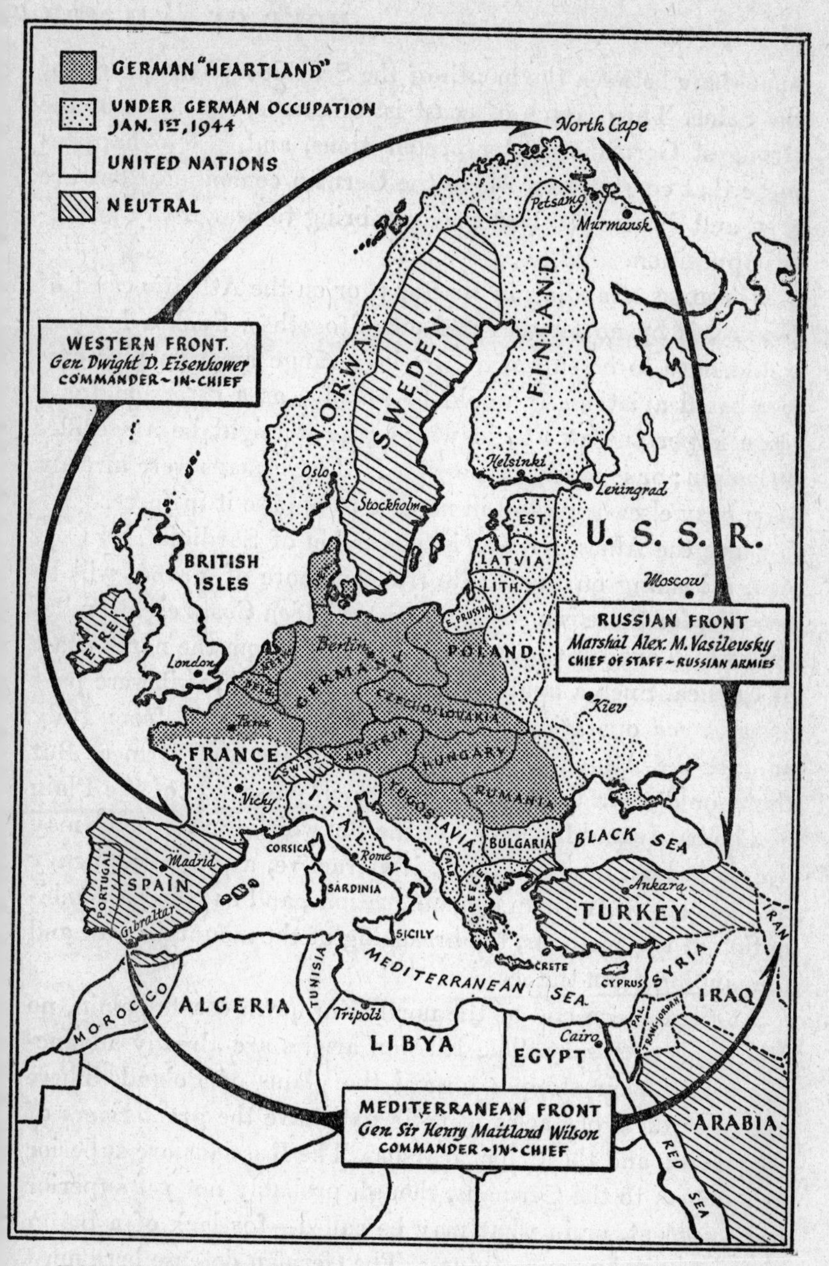

THE EUROPEAN THEATER OF OPERATIONS

somewhere between the mouth of the Scheldt and the mouth of the Seine. This stretch of coast is, of course, the scene of the strongest German counter-preparations, and it also happens to be that coastal area where the German communications are best, and shortest, so that they can bring to bear really powerful opposition.

Of course, a landing in Brittany, or on the Atlantic coast of France, is by no means ruled out altogether. Such a landing would have to be supported by long-range aviation plus carrier-based aviation. It would be possible as a diversion for a more important attack, in which case it might be a sacrifice operation; or it would be possible if the Germans were already very busy elsewhere, and in no case to oppose it in force.

Since the Allies are now in possession of Sardinia and Corsica, a landing on the Mediterranean shore of France will be feasible, for there is a stretch of that Golden Coast eighty miles long which averages only about 115 miles from the north coast of Corsica. Such a landing would be still easier, if it were part of a larger operation which included an assault from Italy against the Alpine passes separating Italy and France. But that would mean that the Allies were in possession of the Plain of Lombardy and the valley of the Po, which the Germans may decide to hold in strength. It is attractive, as imposing heavy burdens on the German communications, and as being a combination of two methods, the breaching of the mountain wall and the landing from the sea.

At the eastern end of the north European coastal plain, no landing is necessary. The Russian armies are already advancing across their steppes toward the plains of Poland. There are no natural obstacles in their path save the great rivers of the region, and the Pripet marshes. The Russians are superior in numbers to the Germans, though probably not yet superior in equipment, or in what may be called—for lack of a better term—tactical resourcefulness. The German defense here must be based on exploiting their superiority in these respects by the use of every artificial device and fortification within the art of their engineers to devise. Rivers form useful obstacles within great fortified systems, and as on the Donetz and the Dnieper, the German defenses will probably tend to follow the courses of the rivers, which in general run perpendicularly to the fronts they must seek to hold. But the shortage of man-power both for labor and fighting, must compel the German planners to seek ever shorter lines, a fact which is favored by the geography of the region. Even eliminating the defense of Finland, the remainder of the 1943 line, from Leningrad to the Black Sea, is more than twice the distance from the Baltic shore to the spurs of the Carpathians. Retiring westward from their former positions, the Germans do so on an ever narrowing total front, and they can even count on this being divided, for defensive purposes, into two separate short fronts by the formidable obstacle of the Pripet marshes.

The southern, or mountain front, the German defenders may consider as divided into three parts. The first is the Alpine front between France and Italy. Next, after the interval formed by neutral Switzerland, comes the mountain wall which divides Italy from Austria and northwestern Jugoslavia. Finally, there is the Balkan front, which presents a series of mountain barriers beginning clear down at the head of the Aegean Sea and stretching back to the final barrier of the Carpathians. The Germans must decide where and how these several fronts will be defended.

In principle, under modern conditions of warfare, it is better to begin the defense of a mountain barrier by defending the approaches to the passes. An advance position, running parallel to the mountain chain, is usually made possible by foothills or other natural features, and can be strengthened by artificial means. This is especially advantageous if, as with the Germans, one of the main objects is to gain time. Such an outpost position compels the enemy to develop a powerful attack under circumstances which often deny him good lateral communications; he may therefore lose some of his freedom of action. If no such position is held, and the enemy is able to move directly upon the passes, a mountain chain is not as formidable a barrier to military movement as it used to be. This the Germans themselves proved, in their Balkan campaign and in Norway. The attacker will always have air superiority—he would not be the attacker if he did not—and if he has good mountain troops he will not only be able to get hold of one or more passes, but he will be able by his air power to interfere with the flexible system of defense which is the only hope of preventing him from passing over. This system depends on keeping strong reserves in hand, to attack when the enemy is, in the military term, astride the pass. A powerful air cover acts here as in forcing a beachhead—it gives the attacking force protection from counter attack until it is firmly established.

In other words, mountain warfare has now become almost as much a warfare of maneuver as warfare in open country, albeit somewhat slower maneuver and by somewhat smaller units. Advantage in such matters as equipment, physical endurance, spirit, leadership of small units, and air support tend, under these conditions, to be of greater proportionate importance in mountain warfare. In all of these, save perhaps leadership of small units, the advantage will be with the Allies. The Germans will, therefore, do well not to place too much reliance in mountains as forming impregnable defenses. Their chief value to the Germans is that they impose delay, because movements in mountainous country are slower, and because of the restrictions on the number and the capacity of the lines of communication. In particular, an army which has passed through a mountainous region, and whose communications with its base remain dependent on the roads and railways of that region, is restricted in numbers to those which can be supplied by these sometimes precarious means.

Applying these principles to the geographical situation on their southern front, it would seem desirable for the Germans to try to hold northern Italy as long as they can, to protect the approaches to the French and Austrian passes. Southern and central Italy are strategic liabilities, and economic liabilities as well for the most part, presuming that the Germans have laid up sufficient reserves of sulphur, lead and zinc. The line of the Etruscan Apennines, roughly from Leghorn to Ancona, offers one possible defense position; the line of the river Po offers a second; and still a third, that of the Piave, is available as far as the approaches of the Brenner Pass and the Austrian frontier are concerned. There is however one disadvantage in giving up southern Italy, not in connection with the Alpine frontier, but as to its possible use by the Allies as a base of operations against the Balkan peninsula.

The Balkan front is a difficult one for the Germans. Probably their most hopeful course is to begin at the beginning, and fight desperately to prevent an Allied lodgment there at all. The Allies now have no foothold in the Balkans. To get an army there, they will have to come in from the sea, and to do that they will have to begin by reducing the island outposts which command the approaches to the Aegean Sea, which in turn is the avenue to Salonika—the gateway of the Vardar-Morava valley, the only practicable approach to the heart of the Balkan peninsula which an invading Allied army can use under existing circumstances. The reduction of Crete, with its strong fortifications and its picked German garrison, may prove more troublesome than the reduction of Sicily, especially as the Allied bases are not as close as Tunisia, Malta and Pantelleria are to Sicily. Hence an approach seems probable by way of Cyprus to Castelorizzo to Rhodes. Rhodes is, indeed, in many ways the key to the Aegean, and the chink in the armor of Crete.

Once the outposts are driven in, so to speak, the German situation in the Balkan peninsula becomes more difficult at each step. The Allies are in Southern Italy; if they can establish themselves also in the Aegean Islands, they can do, immediately, two things: they can start sending supplies and reinforcements across the Adriatic Sea to the Dalmatian ports of Yugoslavia, and they can start transforming the Aegean Islands into air bases and supply depots for a landing at Salonika. It is difficult—though not impossible—to send an army of invasion across the Adriatic Sea from Italy, because of the small capacity of the seaports of Yugoslavia, and the fact that their communications with the interior run through the terrific passes of the Dinaric Alps, being thus limited to a very few roads, and to a couple of narrow-gauge railways. These would be insufficient for the supply of a large army trying to fight its way into the interior. But already in that interior are many brave, tough fighting men who need only weapons and direction to become formidable enemies of the German forces of occupation: provided they can be unified. These Yugoslav patriot armies control considerable portions of the country as it is. If they could be supplied with light automatic arms, grenades, explosives, portable radios, light mortars, and reinforcements in the shape of specially trained units of mountain artillery, engineers, signal troops and perhaps a few detachments of small fast tanks, they could give the Germans far more trouble than they are now doing, if they would only unite against the Germans and stop fighting each other. With proper air cooperation, they might be able to cut the Belgrade-Nis-Salonika railway and keep it cut. If this were done, the Germans would have trouble in making a defense at and around Salonika. And certainly it would take a great many German troops to keep that railway guarded.

With the Serbs in arms, and with Salonika taken, the Germans must eventually withdraw to the line of the Danube and the Sava, and on that line they must stand. If they fail to make that stand good, they lose the Rumanian oil fields, and one half their oil supply, permanently. They risk the turning of the line of the Dniester, and a junction between the Allied right and the Russian left somewhere on the Moldavian plain. When these things happen, Germany is in a bad way.

There are two other factors in the defensive strategy of Germany. One is the question of defense against air attack. That has two phases—the building up of physical defenses, and the keeping of Allied air bases at a distance. In the west, Allied bases cannot approach nearer than they are now as long as there is no landing. On the east, the Russians—whose strong point has never been strategical bombing—can be allowed to come quite a bit nearer than they are now without undue risk, though the industrial district of Silesia must be protected at all costs. On the south, however, the Germans cannot allow the establishment of Allied air bases in the Plain of Lombardy if they are to keep inviolate their Czech and Austrian industrial regions, which hitherto, like Silesia, have gone comparatively untouched. The Germans must also turn the whole attention of their aircraft industry to the turning out of fighters in increasing numbers, and they must increase the capacity of plants not in easy reach of our bombing raids. If they can, despite our bombers, bring up the scale of their fighter production, they may begin to make the bombings more expensive. A very considerable increase in the scale of anti-aircraft protection for key industrial centers seems also certain, and will be one of the possibilities opened up by a reduction in the extent of occupied territory, the length of the fronts and the length of the lines of communication. The less mobile field artillery that is required, the more anti-aircraft artillery can be provided.

The remaining factor to be considered is naval strategy. The

Germans have up to this time placed great reliance in their U-boat campaign, for the purpose of diminishing the eastward flow of American fighting power in all its forms. For a time, they enjoyed a considerable degree of success. Now there are signs that the U-boat is being dealt with. The U-boats are being countered at sea by Allied escort craft and aircraft; and their bases, and the shipyards and industrial centers where U-boats, engines and parts are manufactured are being smashed by bombing attack. It may be that the Germans will be able to renew this campaign by shifting the building of U-boats to Baltic ports, and by technical improvements making existing U-boats more effective. But this seems doubtful. The Germans will be in no position to continue to waste their substance on doubtful weapons the moment that the cost of those weapons in labor and material becomes greater than the results achieved by them. Should the Germans be compelled to decide to abandon the U-boat campaign, one effect on their strategy would be a diminished interest in the Atlantic ports of Norway and France.

As for the German surface fleet, it is possible that more of its heavy units may be sacrificed (as was the *Scharnhorst*) in a desperate attack on the shipping which is bringing to Europe the power that turns the balance against Germany. The remainder will be required to protect the left flank of the German army, on the Baltic Sea, as the retirement from Russia develops. Such units of the Italian fleet as remain in German possession may be used in the Adriatic, based on Pola, to prevent the Allies from having it all their own way in transporting supplies to the Yugoslav patriots, or may even find some employment in the Aegean.

One final set of considerations—political considerations—remains to be taken into account. We have already dealt with the political conditions inside Germany and her occupied, conquered territories, but there are two other categories of states to be considered: the German satellites, and the neutrals.

As for the satellites, we can almost rule out Finland at once. That nation is so anxious to be out of the war, and so difficult for the Germans to defend, that its abandonment by them is almost a foregone conclusion. It is no longer worth its price to the Germans, especially in view of the pressing need for a withdrawal in Russia.

Bulgaria is in inner turmoil. Her people are well aware of the misery that resulted from their having backed the wrong horse in the last war. They are not happy to find themselves opposed to Russia again. They are still less happy to find themselves far out on the end of what must seem to them a very long limb, exposed to the first blast of Allied attack on the Balkan peninsula, and with a very uncertain neighbor in Turkey. It will hardly be going too far to say that in Bulgaria, the Germans have a satellite which will switch to another planetary center the moment it gets a chance. And the Bulgars still retain some powers of decision because of their geographical location and because their army is still intact. The Rumanians and the Hungarians are in very much less independent positions. Both of them have been sadly weakened by their losses in Russia, the Rumanians in particular. They hate each other cordially. They are well aware that they have nothing to hope for from the Germans. But they are trapped. There is no escape for them until Allied armies crash across their borders. The Slovaks are in a very similar position. The Croat *Ustashis*, alone of the German satellites, are in the miserable state of those for whom there is no repentance. They are finding troops to replace Italian garrisons in Serbia and Dalmatia, because they must sink or swim with their German masters.

The neutral states of Europe may profoundly affect the German strategy. If any of them ceases to be neutral, the results will be considerable. Two of them, Sweden and Turkey, have already taken a decidedly pro-Allied slant; to these may be added Portugal. Sweden will probably not enter the war unless compelled; the compulsion may come with an Allied invasion of Norway, which might force the Germans to demand the use of Swedish railways to reinforce her garrisons on the Norwegian coast. Sweden has already stopped the so-called "normal" transit of German troops and military stores over her lines, imposing a heavy additional strain on German coastal shipping. If for any reason Sweden becomes a belligerent, the Germans will have all they can do to find means to deal with the well armed, well-equipped Swedish forces; and unless they do deal with those forces successfully and swiftly, they will find a northern air front opened against them that will come close to being disastrous.

As for Turkey, that state controls two situations of the utmost importance—the historic Straits connecting the Aegean and Black Seas, and the only non-German foothold in the Balkan peninsula. If the Straits are opened to Allied shipping, the western Allies will have a short and capacious supply route to Russia so far superior to the long round-about trip to the Arctic ports or through the Persian Gulf as to beggar comparison. If Turkey becomes an active belligerent, the way is opened to by-pass Salonika and its mountains, and strike directly into Bulgaria and toward the Danube Valley and the Rumanian oilfields.

It is important to note that Sweden and Turkey—the two neutrals whose joining in the war would most benefit the Allies, and most injure Germany—both cherish historic fears of the Russians. The Swedes fear Russian domination of the Baltic, and also a possible Russian demand for a port on the open Atlantic, with access to it through Swedish territory. They are strongly opposed to Russian subjection of Finland. The Turks are anxious over possible Russian claims to the Straits, an ancient focal point of Russian ambitions. This is one reason why, the moment it becomes even reasonably safe to do so, the Turks will probably open the Straits in the hope of winning general favor among the United Nations, Russia included, even if they do not join in the war.

Portugal, the historic ally of Britain, is now beginning to be relieved of fears of invasion by German armies coming through Spain. This has resulted in Portugal's action in giving us the free use of the Azores Islands for anti-submarine operations—an accession which may be decisive in the Atlantic, as permitting far more flexible use of our submarine-hunting aircraft than is now possible.

The present government of Spain can certainly not be said to have pro-Allied leanings, and the desire of most of the Spanish people is certainly to stay out of the war altogether. However, Spain does afford access to France which might be far less costly than a landing operation. The time may come when political changes in Spain will make this possible.

Switzerland is in the center of Europe, controlling important railway lines linking Germany with Italy. Historically neutral, the Swiss will certainly defend that neutrality; they cannot be expected to do more. Swiss neutrality may seem important to some of the Nazi leaders as affording them a possible haven, if not from Allied vengeance, at least from worse and closer dangers to their lives. Germany would have little to gain at this late date in challenging the hardy Swiss in their mountain stronghold.

We thus come to an end of a rather lengthy survey of the strategic position of Germany, as that nation turns to defensive warfare.

To summarize: The German strategy from this time on must be a defensive strategy, a delaying strategy, whose object is to gain time—time for the United Nations to sicken of the bloodshed, time for dissensions to arise among them, time for political shifts of power in Germany itself which may make possible the gaining of better terms. The German heartland, without which they cannot go on fighting, may be described as the territory of Germany itself, western and central Poland, Denmark, Czechoslovakia, Hungary, Rumania, northern Yugoslavia, Austria, Luxemburg, Belgium, the Netherlands and part of northern France. This central and vital area must be held. Once it is invaded, the beginning of the end is at hand, and the end itself not too far away.

It is, of course, a much smaller area than the Germans now hold. In Russia, they have already found themselves compelled to give up much of their former conquests. They may have to give up more, perhaps in a further strategic withdrawal in great depth and on a broad front. Finland they may also have to abandon, and the peninsula of Italy. But the rest—Norway, western and southern France, the Aegean Islands, the southern Balkans, northern Italy, the Crimea and some other sections of western Russia—may very well be the scene of furious delaying actions, in which the German object will be to exact heavy Allied losses without paying too great a price themselves. They will try to keep their positions well consolidated and linked up. They will hope to make use of the forces saved by their various withdrawals to organize powerful reserve armies, centrally located so as to be able to counter-attack in force to cover further withdrawal of advanced elements and to check Allied thrusts which go too far. They are unlikely again to take the risk of pushing out very large forces into distant positions, as they did at Stalingrad and in Tunisia, with the result that these forces were cut off and destroyed. And they will have to abandon the offensive in the air in order to purchase, at that price, increased defensive power. They may also have to abandon their offensive at sea.

The defeat of Germany will come to pass when the German heartland, as above described, can no longer be defended.

In all probability, that will be brought about by a combination of the methods open to the United Nations: by external blockade; by air attacks on German industries and communications, which may be called internal blockade; and by the advance of Allied armies converging from the outer perimeter of the German defense system upon its central and vital area.

In the course of all these operations, there will arise a series of political problems which will have to be solved, and the solution of which demands unity of policy among the United Nations. These problems will arise in connection with enemy or enemy-satellite states, such as Italy, Bulgaria, Finland, Rumania, Hungary, and Croatia. They will arise in connection with states now neutral, such as Sweden, Turkey, and perhaps Portugal, Spain and Switzerland. They will arise in connection with states now occupied by the enemy, but which may be freed by our invasion or his forced withdrawal, such as France, Belgium, the Netherlands, Norway, Denmark, Yugoslavia, Poland, Greece and Czechoslovakia. The complexity and difficulty of these problems we need not attempt to describe. The mere listing of the states to which they apply is a sufficient warning.

As long as the territory of a satellite state, or of any Allied state formerly occupied by the enemy, is in whole or in part the scene of military operations, or controls important military communications upon which Allied forces depend, the military requirements must prevail—and the first of these is that order must be maintained. As for satellite territory, there must be Allied military government, or there must be a local government capable of maintaining order which has the approval of the Allied powers, or at least of the particular powers whose forces are operating in that area. As to rescued territory, it means in general either that the recognized "government in exile" returns and takes over, or, as may well happen, that the people set up a new government which suits them better, and can keep order. This can be very simply stated, as a matter of general principle; but like so many simple principles, these are not easy to apply.

The moment we prepare to hand over civil control to any authority whatever, other than our own military, we run into trouble with everyone who does not happen to like that particular government or its personnel. Everywhere there will be a contest for power; everywhere there will be claimants of greater or less degree who will be courting our favor, or clamoring for our support; everywhere there will be old grudges to pay off. Decisions of this sort cannot be left to the military; generals have no training which fits them for such tasks. These are political decisions, and they must be made by statesmen after a thorough examination of all the conditions. It is all very well to say that in any case these are decisions which affect only the temporary establishment of civil governments, which will presently be replaced with permanent governments when the time comes. That is not the point. Whenever we give even temporary support to any such government, we are writing with indelible ink on the pages of the future. The steps we take can never be wholly retraced, and if we take the wrong steps we shall be building up for ourselves, and for our hopes of peace, a legacy of future troubles. At best we cannot hope for a perfect record. Mistakes will be made, our motives will be misconstrued, deliberately or otherwise; and if there is not a general agreement among all the great Powers concerned, the conditions behind the lines of our advancing armies are likely to become chaotic.

Likewise, it is apparent that under the conditions given for the defeat of Germany, a much greater degree of military unity will be necessary, as between the western Powers and Russia, than has hitherto prevailed. In the Balkans particularly, we may see Russian forces cooperating directly with British and American forces. The closest coordination of effort will be required, will indeed be indispensable in order to bring the war to an end at the earliest possible moment.

When that moment comes, it is likewise indispensable that the military authorities of the Powers, who will impose armistice terms or at least be responsible for immediate security measures, shall be in full agreement. The surrendering enemy forces must be disarmed. Irresponsible acts of vengeance must, as far as possible, be checked once resistance has ceased. Order must be maintained in enemy territory. The persons of enemy leaders must be secured. Zones of occupation must be allotted to the various Allied forces concerned. It is, of course, to be hoped that no part of Germany shall escape complete occupation by United Nations troops. In this, as in all else, there must be unity, previous agreement, amongst the Allied governments. If we permit the necessity for making vital decisions to overtake us without such previous agreement, the most disastrous results may follow.

Presuming, however, that we have such agreement, what will be the state of affairs in Europe when the Germans are finally beaten to their knees in defeat?

First, there will be present in Europe powerful armies of United Nations troops. In Eastern Europe, the majority of these troops will be Russian. It may be that the bulk of the Russian troops will be under purely Russian command. But the rest of the Allied forces in Europe will be composite. They will include British and American troops, and troops of the British Dominions. They will likewise include French and Polish troops. They may include Turkish troops. They may include troops belonging to any of the liberated United Nations which there has been opportunity to organize. They will be international armies, serving under inter-Allied commanders selected by agreement among the Powers concerned. They will be, with the exception of the Russians, under the high direction of the Combined Chiefs of Staff functioning dually at Washington and London, and, it is to be hoped, in very close relationship by that time with the Russian High Command. The staffs of these armies will include officers of various nationalities, who will have become accustomed to working together and will have grown to trust and appreciate each other.

The same thing is true of air forces, which will, under the highest military command, be integrated with the armies and will be operating in the closest coordination with them. The supply systems, depots, lines of communication, hospitals, and other establishments of all these forces will be jointly operated under the direction of administrative staffs on which British, American, French and other officers will be serving, just as is the case with the inter-Allied staffs in England and the Mediterranean area at this moment.

Europe will be a wreck, almost a desert in its central portions. Recovery will have begun, probably, at the edges—it is astonishing how swiftly human beings begin to build again when war has done its worst and passed them by—but the greater part of the task will be yet to do.

On the east, Russia will be already at work on her great task of reconstruction. On the west, the British will stand firmly, their industries in operation, their economy on strict rations but in good working order. Switzerland in the center will be a little island of order and civilization. Possibly Sweden will be, too. Spain and Portugal, far off to the southwest, will be a sort of by-passed area. But for the rest, there will be just two kinds of lands in Europe—those through which the war has passed as we close in on the enemy, and those which the enemy's surrender, or collapse, has just delivered into our hands.

In the first category may be France, Italy, most of the Balkan Peninsula, parts of Poland, Norway, and perhaps other countries. In the second category will be the central territory which the Germans will seek to hold to the last—Germany, and the immediately surrounding countries. How much of it they will still hold when the end comes, no one can foretell. Probably a good deal.

In the liberated land—whether that liberation has been from the German yoke as conqueror, or the German yoke as "senior partner"—there will be some sort of government for the maintenance of order, for the distribution of relief, and for the making of a beginning at the restoration of normal conditions of life. The nature of that government will vary with the locality, the character of the inhabitants, the degree of devastation, and the military importance of the area in the attack on Germany. For all these governments, or quasi-governments, the United Nations as a whole, the prosecutors of the war, will bear some measure of responsibility. None of them could exist without our sanction, and in some measure our support. In some parts, there will still be military governments directly administered by our officers. Almost everywhere, there will be the operations of the United Nations Relief and Rehabilitation Administration, seeking to provide food and shelter for the hungry and the homeless, to care for the aged, the sick, and the children, and to provide the means (seed, tools, animals) by which the production of food may again begin.

In Germany, there will be millions of sullen, defeated people who have lost all heart and all hope. Most of them will be under-nourished physically, and broken in spirit from the pitiless hail of bombs and from the Nazi terror. What horrors internal strife, or the vengeance of the insulted and injured, may have perpetrated, we cannot now imagine. It is altogether possible that the one remaining emotion in German hearts will be hate—a hate which may be divided between those who have brought the German nation to this sorry pass, and those who have inflicted on them all the resultant horrors of war.

Who will speak for these people? From whom, when the end comes, can we accept surrender? Or if it comes by utter collapse, with whom can we arrange the terms under which the surviving Germans must live while our occupation continues? Will it be the Nazis? Surely not. The military chiefs, then? Or some new government, rising suddenly to power? Or just local authorities in each town and district, or those who may have taken authority unto themselves, for lack of anyone else to do it? We do not know. But it is abundantly clear that we must have a united policy on all these points, that this policy must be flexible, adaptable to changes in conditions as these changes occur—which means that there must be some agency common to all the United Nations where such changes can be duly considered.

In all Europe, there will be only one real kind of power that will count, for the moment: the armed might of the United Nations. That power, and the nations whose instrument and symbol it is, will have a tremendous responsibility. They will have to lay the foundations for the rebuilding of European civilization; and the new fabric of that civilization will, or will not, be firmly established according to whether the foundation is well and truly and wisely and carefully laid.

We Americans can never, at the bar of history or even in our own hearts, escape our share of that terrible responsibility. This time we cannot dare to say, any one of us, "Am I my brother's keeper?" For each one of us, each nation of the United Nations is in very truth his brother's keeper.

I leave then in your minds the thought of this Europe the day after the Germans are beaten—this Europe with all its millions of men, women, and children, who will need food and shelter and medicine and all the rest of the things we can give them only temporarily, but who will need most of all—hope.

There will be work to do in Europe, work which we can only begin, which these others must then carry on for themselves. But there will be yet another task before us when that day of German surrender comes, before we can settle down to the building of our brave new world. That task will be the defeat of Japan, and while Europe is rising from her ashes, the armed power of the United Nations must turn to Asia.

7. THE DEFEAT OF JAPAN

THERE IS NOTHING certain about war.

But it seems altogether probable that the war against Japan will still be in progress when Germany is beaten.

If it is, the hour that Germany acknowledges defeat will be an hour of great danger for America and for the United Nations.

Anyone who remembers the last Armistice, the hysterical crowds, the mad rejoicing, the instant cry among the American and Dominion soldiery "We wanna go home!"—and the wave of joy that swept across the country as fathers and mothers, wives and sweethearts realized that their dear ones had been spared—anyone who remembers all that, will understand what the first reaction will be when the news comes that Germany has capitulated. The preceding strain will be a great one, for the Germans will fight hard, and our losses will be far heavier than any we suffered in the last war. We must be on our guard against the reaction that may follow the defeat of Germany, if Japan is still in arms against us when that takes place.

The Japanese are counting on just that moment. They, like the Germans, know that they are beaten. Like the Germans, their one hope is to make their final defeat cost us so dearly that we will stop somewhere short of making that defeat complete. Their military weapons may purchase them delay, but are insufficient to save them in the end. They will resort to political and psychological weapons, and they will use them with great cunning.

The moment the Germans are through, the Japanese are likely to fling a peace offer at our heads. It may be a surprisingly far-reaching offer. It may even include the giving up of all their conquered territory in the Philippines, the Netherlands Indies, Burma, Malaya, and the Pacific Islands, or such of that territory as they then still hold: also the evacuation of Thailand and French Indo China; and a complete withdrawal from all China except, probably, Manchukuo. In other words, the Japanese may offer to return to the *status quo ante* of 1931.

The purpose behind this peace offer will be to avoid a military defeat which could never be explained to the Japanese people, with their belief in the divinity of their Emperor. Its underlying motive will be precisely that of the German war lords—to get a chance to try again, later on, when Japan's enemies have forgotten, and disarmed, and gone back to their peaceful pursuits. The Japanese count on seeing the Philippines given independence, on political turmoil in India, Burma, Malaya and the Netherlands Indies. They think that later on all these countries may become easy prey, with economic advances first and military reconquest later. And as for China, they know that China will be a long time in building up her political unity and anything like a real industrial capacity, they count on China as a tremendous market for Japanese manufactured products, and they think that eventually, when they are again in control of all the islands which command the sea routes to China, they will be in a position effectively to control that great country even if they have not been able to conquer it by force of arms.

The one thing the Japanese leaders cannot stand the thought of is being decisively and unmistakably beaten now, by the irresistible combination of force which is in arms against them and will be able to devote its undivided attention to them as soon as Germany is disposed of. They cannot foresee what may happen when their armies have been beaten in their distant outposts, when their fleet has been swept from the seas, when their merchant shipping has ceased to exist, when their war plants no longer have iron or oil or copper and when the whole coast of the Asiatic continent is one great air base from which they are being battered into a submission which they will then lack any means to avert. When these things happen, the Japanese leaders know that the whole moral and spiritual foundations of the Japanese people may crumble. These foundations depend on no mere legend of invincibility resting on one man, and on the experience of a few years. They are formed of an ingrained belief in the divine origins of the Emperor and his long line of predecessors, stretching back into "ages eternal." What will happen when the fact of defeat stares the Japanese people in the face, is something their leaders do not dare to contemplate; for with that defeat at the hands of mere human beings, and despised western barbarians at that, any belief in the divine origin of the Emperor and his descendants must vanish from the mind of the dullest Japanese peasant. And what then? On whom will the Japanese people turn, in their suffering and fury and despair? Will the Empire of the Rising Sun disappear, drowned in the blood of its own maddened inhabitants, in one awful outburst of civil strife? It is altogether possible.

And even if this does not happen, these Japanese leaders well know that a defeated Japan will never be left in any position to renew her criminal career of conquest for a long time to come, if at all. They know that she will be, at least, completely disarmed, deprived of every outpost position, driven altogether off the continent of Asia, and reduced to the status of a secondary power, with neither influence nor authority.

So they will seize upon any opportunity that offers to make a proposal of peace. The defeat of Germany will give them a really outstanding opportunity, for they can then propose peace and still save "face." They can pose as noble benefactors of mankind. They can say: "We have found that we are misunderstood by the peoples among whom we have gone to bring them the matchless benefits of our 'co-prosperity sphere.' Very well. We will withdraw. We will take our troops, our ships, our airplanes home again. We will ask nothing save our boundaries and protectorates as of 1931. We offer peace to the world, that peace of which all nations are so desperately in need. We have not been defeated, we cannot be defeated if we go on fighting. But we are not insensible to the claims of humanity. Let the world be at peace."

That will be a difficult plea to resist. But if we of the United Nations do not resist it, we shall know no real peace at all. The Japanese will simply be bowing to inexorable circumstance, and biding their time, meanwhile keeping in hand their weapons and preparing themselves for another try when the time is ripe. They will be making a strategic retreat, as they did from Siberia and Shantung after the last war. There will be no abandonment of criminal purpose. Presently, they will move forward once more, tentatively, a small move here and a small move there, never enough at any one time to provoke drastic action against them—until they are again ready for some major challenge, perhaps to Russia, perhaps to the United States, perhaps to Britain.

Let us never forget that this is a peoples' war—a war whose objective, whose only possible worthwhile objective, is the restoration of peace, a lasting peace which shall give civilization the breathing space it needs. It is not enough to accept a mere truce, on the enemy's terms, however attractive they may seem.

With the Japanese there can be no peace as long as they have arms in their hands and a chance to try again when our backs are turned. Their objectives are not ours, nor are they those of the vast majority of the people of this world. Their habits of thought, their traditions, stem directly out of the Middle Ages, from which they emerged within the memory of men still living.

Let us remember, also, that if we are to have a world ruled by law, that law must be based on essential justice if it is to endure. It is not justice to let a red-handed criminal go unwhipped of the law, because it may seem convenient to do so. It is not justice to the millions of Eastern peoples over whom an armed Japan will hang an eternal menace, to allow the Japanese to keep in their hands the weapons which, as they have amply proved, they know how to use only as instruments of conquest and oppression. It is not justice to ourselves, to require that we shall maintain forever a scale of armament corresponding to that which the Japanese see fit to maintain.

When Germany is finished, there can be no temporizing with the Japanese. The full power of the United Nations will be mobilized and ready. We shall have veteran armies, navies and air forces, prepared to strike. We shall have vast depots of military stores, and war industries to keep them full. We shall have experienced commanders and staffs. Never again—in all probability—shall we be so well prepared to deal with the menace of Japan.

That opportunity must not be thrown away.

What the military situation in the Far East will be, when the moment of German defeat comes, cannot of course be predicted with any accuracy. But the general outlines of the course which the war against Japan must take, can be foreseen to some extent.

In order to construct those outlines, we must examine the conditions under which Japan is fighting.

Like the Germans, the Japanese now stand on the defensive.

Their reserves of raw materials, and in particular their painfully constructed and long-trained air force, have been largely exhausted by their offensive effort which began at Pearl Harbor and came to an end with the failure of their feeble stabs at Ceylon, at Port Moresby, at Midway and at Dutch Harbor. Having reached the limits of their offensive power, they are now seeking to digest their spoil; to replace, from the resources of their captured territory, the loss of the imports by which their industry was formerly sustained. That they have not been able to do more than they have along these lines is due to the fact that they have not been left in peace to make these adjustments and replacements. They have constantly been subjected to the strain and stress of war. Neither in Burma, nor in China, nor on their vast Pacific front, have they known a moment's relaxation. They gambled on a short war and a long period of respite and reconstruction. They have failed, and their leaders know perfectly well that their only hope now lies in a defense that shall cost the United Nations so dearly as to win terms for the Japanese which will leave them with means to try again.

From the United Nations viewpoint, the war against Japan is a war of different military character than that against Germany. It is very largely, though not altogether, an amphibious war. It makes enormous demands on shipping, and it requires powerful naval forces of all categories, air forces, and highly trained amphibious shock troops. Its ultimate demands for large ground armies may grow as the war develops, but these demands are not great in its initial stages, except in China.

The war against Japan may be divided into three periods. The first, that of the enemy offensive, has already passed. The second, the stage in which the United Nations pass to the limited offensive and undertake preparatory moves in making ready for decisive blows, is now in progress. The third will come when it is possible for decisive blows to be struck directly at Japan's vital centers. This third period may come when Germany's downfall permits us to turn in full strength against Japan. It may begin before that, but if it does it will be greatly accelerated by the end of the war in Europe. In all probability, that event will be the turning point of the war in the Pacific, and it is toward that event that all the measures now being taken by the Japanese, and against them, may be said to be preparatory.

The factor of distance governs the war against Japan in all its phases. The centers of Japanese power lie many thousands of miles from the centers of power of Britain, the United States or Russia, while China is not capable without support of launching a powerful offensive of its own. In order to get at Japan, the fighting power of the United Nations must be brought to bases in the Far East over long and painful lines of communication, the very maintenance of which absorbs much of the energy which passes along them, leaving only a marginal strength to be employed at the farther end. The Japanese for their part have thrust themselves out in every possible direction, to seize outposts very far away from their vital centers, and it is on this far flung perimeter that they are now fighting desperate delaying actions.

Their principal weakness is in the air. For their sudden offensive which began at Pearl Harbor, they had carefully built up a strong, well-trained air force. They had accumulated a large number of planes, and they had trained their crews over a period of years until they had a weapon of truly formidable power. But behind it, there did not exist the ability to replace and go on replacing which is the essential foundation of air power. Their utmost efforts cannot produce more than 600 to 1000 aircraft of all types each month, of which not more than one-half are of combat types. And it takes much longer to train a Japanese to be a competent pilot than it does to train an American or an Australian or an Englishman. The Japanese used their accumulated air power lavishly, even recklessly, to support their offensive. It was sufficient to win their immediate objectives, but it exhausted itself in doing so. And since then they have been hustled so rudely and continuously that they have not had time to build anew. The result is apparent in all that they now try to do.

On every front, they suffer very heavy losses because urgent necessity compels them to use pilots who are insufficiently trained, and who are further handicapped by being given inferior machines. The Japanese have never had time to switch the production of their factories to newer models which take into account the tactical lessons the war has taught. No really new model of Japanese aircraft has appeared since the beginning of the war, while we are constantly feeding new models into our combat squadrons. In many cases the Japanese have been found using entirely obsolete models against our newest and best. The effect of this is cumulative; the qualitative gap between Japan's air force and ours slowly widens. Already the Japanese are unable to accomplish their missions, and can take the air at all only at prohibitive cost. Probably they are holding back some of their best planes and pilots for the defense of their home centers, and we shall encounter more serious opposition as we approach those centers. But in the outpost areas, the Japanese air strength is already a broken reed.

At sea, the Japanese still hold in reserve their powerful battle fleet. They have probably strengthened this force by the conversion of several of the larger ships under construction from battleships or cruisers to aircraft carriers, after the battles of the Coral Sea, Midway and the Solomon Islands had practically wiped out their original carrier strength. In the cruiser and destroyer categories, they have suffered very heavily. These losses have arisen most particularly from the curious Japanese practice of persistently sending small task forces into areas dominated by our sea and air power, in frantic endeavors to relieve their army garrisons. They did this from the very outset of the Solomons operations; they did it at Buna, in New Guinea; they did it in the Aleutians; and they kept on doing it in the central Solomons. This practise amounts to the wasting away of the fleet in driblets, for no compensatory gain. It does not make sense from any Occidental point of view; but perhaps it makes sense as against the Japanese background, and considering their immediate objective, which can no longer be to conquer, but to win delay, respite, breathing space to retain the ability to conquer later on. So considered, this naval policy fits in well with the desperate last-ditch battles to which we have become so accustomed when encountering Japanese troops on land. "The Japanese will fight to the last man"—that phrase has become almost a household word in America and England. Perhaps it has become so by deliberate Japanese design.

The Japanese no more than any other people contemplate self-immolation with pleasurable anticipation. They prefer to live, if they can. Perhaps that is why they fight these desperate little battles of the perimeter, at the expenses of their ability to defend the center against all the concentrated force of the United Nations, convinced that their only hope is to impress us now with their powers of individual resistance, their determination to die rather than yield. If they can do that now, while our main power is still in Europe, while they are not really in great danger, then perhaps when the moment of danger does come they will be able to stave it off with a peace offer, which we may accept because we will think the cost of not accepting it too great.

Thus with the Japanese as with others, political and military policy may go hand in hand, and the events of the war may be made to serve the deeper purposes at which the Japanese leaders are aiming.

We have already observed that the war against Japan naturally divides itself into three parts, the first of which (the

Japanese offensive) is now concluded, the second being the containing of Japan while Germany is being defeated, and the third being the all-out offensive against Japan when Germany has been disposed of.

The second period of the war, in which we are now engaged, may gradually blend into the third; that is, as German resistance weakens it may be found possible to step up the offensive against Japan until it assumes the aspect of full-scale assault. This second period does, however, require certain preliminary operations, which involve breaking into the Japanese defensive perimeter by attacks at various points—coordinated attacks, which the Japanese will have difficulty in meeting at all points because of their dwindling resources. Just as with Germany, the ultimate object is the absorption of the Japanese reserves, both of men and of fighting material, so that when the decisive attacks come the Japanese will be unable to deal with them.

The immediate objectives of our initial attacks in the second period may be further analyzed as follows:

(1) To bring aid and comfort to the Chinese.

(2) To sever the sea-lanes which connect the Japanese outposts with their central sources of power and Japanese industries with their outlying sources of raw materials.

(3) To whittle down Japanese sea and air forces and merchant shipping.

(4) To liberate captured territory from Japanese rule.

(5) To bring Allied air power closer to the vital centers of Japan, in preparation for the decisive period of the war.

(6) To keep the Japanese fighting power fully occupied so that the Japanese can neither attempt any effective counterblows, nor launch any new attacks on China or Siberia.

The first of these purposes is perhaps in point of time the most important. Our Chinese allies have suffered untold miseries during seven years of war. The help they have received from outside has not amounted to very much; yet they have kept on fighting. It is not in human nature to endure forever, nor forever to retain confidence in a leadership which can offer no present relief, but only promises for a future whose hopes are so long delayed as in very truth to make the heart sick. It seems therefore very likely, that the continuance of Chinese resistance may be staked on the ability of the allies of China to begin at least preliminary operations for the recovery of Burma during the winter of 1943-1944.

The creation of the Southeast Asia Command as an inter-allied military unit, and the appointment to it of the young and energetic Admiral Lord Louis Mountbatten as Commander-in-Chief, are unquestionably the results of recognition of these Chinese necessities by the governments of the United States and Great Britain, and by the time these words are in print it seems altogether possible that Mountbatten will be making his first moves.

The land routes from India into Burma are of such difficulty and low capacity as to be totally incapable of supplying a large army, though they can permit the passage of guerrilla bands—which the British have been using in Burma with much success. The main invasion force will have to come by sea, which means across the Bay of Bengal from India and Ceylon. This means that both air and naval superiority will have to be established in the Bay of Bengal, and that advance air bases—probably in the Andaman Islands and at Akyab—will have to be taken in order to provide close tactical air support for the landing forces.

The main line of Japanese communications for their troops in Burma is the sea route through the Strait of Malacca, around the tip of the Malay Peninsula. It is the longest sea-lane which the Japanese must deal with. They are undoubtedly trying to supplement it by opening roads from Thailand into Burma, but the terrain difficulties are appalling, and it may

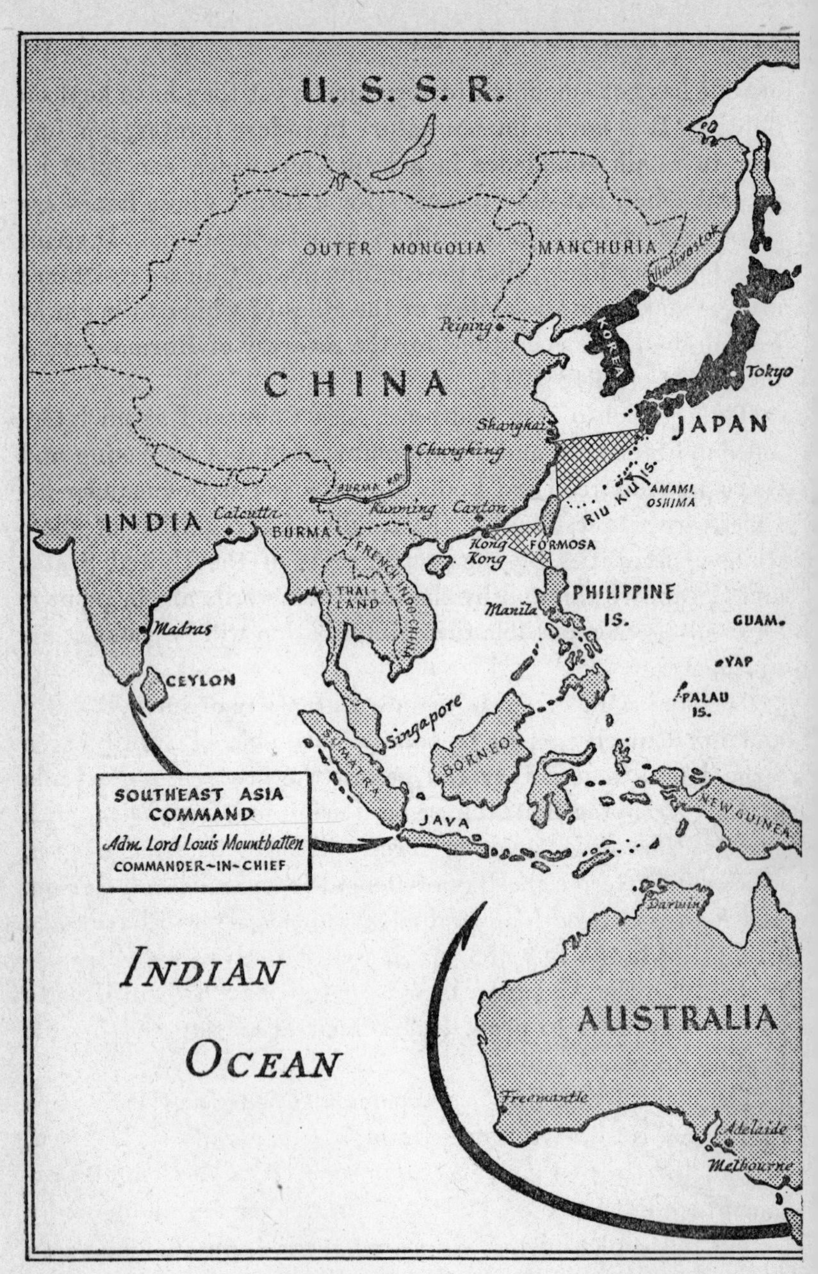

THE PACIFIC AND FAR-EASTERN

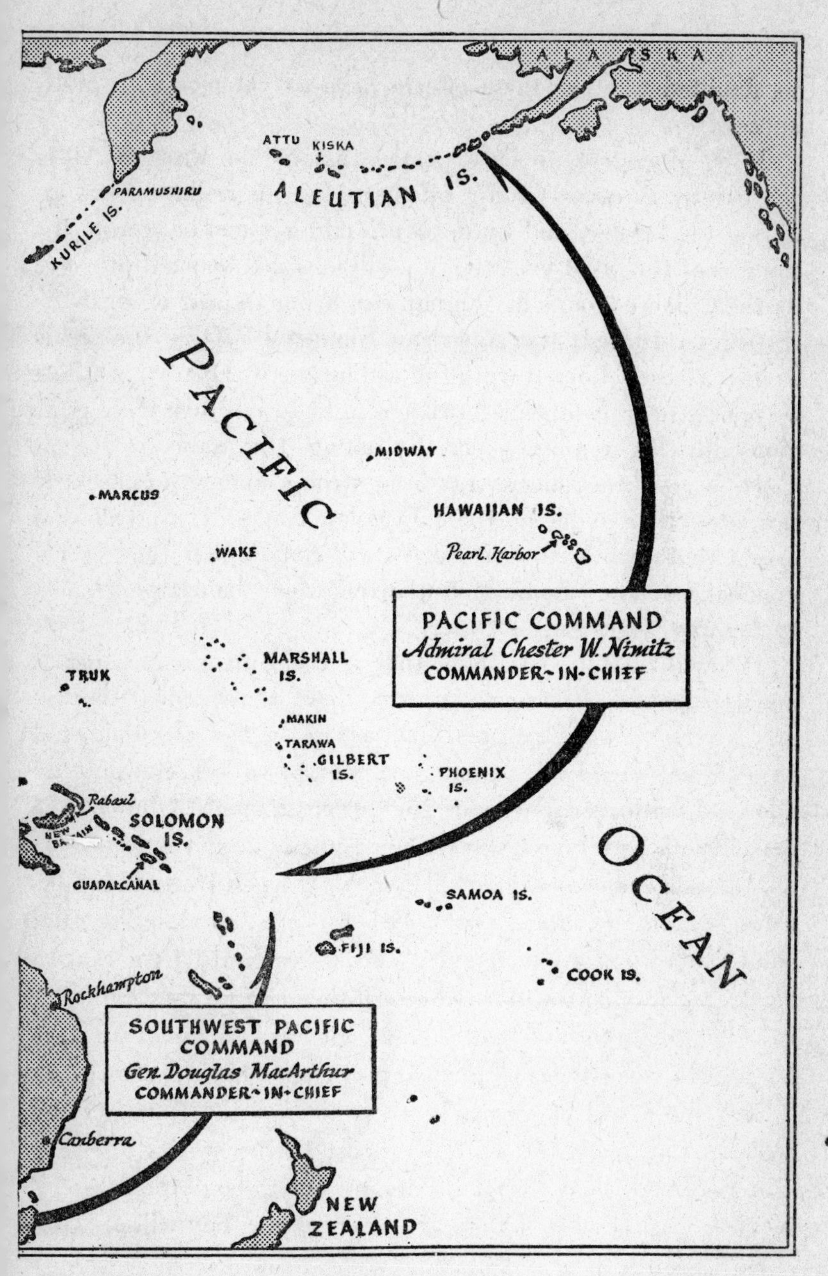

THEATERS OF OPERATIONS

be doubted whether these efforts have as yet met with much success.

It is, of course, to be expected that as the western Allies move into Burma—by air offensive, by guerrilla operations across the border, and by a main landing somewhere near the mouths of the great rivers—they will be aided by such pressure as the Chinese troops in Yunnan can bring to bear against the Japanese. Indeed, the American command in this theater is known as the China-Burma-India Theater of Operations. The Japanese have from time to time sought to improve their positions in this region, especially along the Salween River; Chinese resistance has so far been strong enough to check, if not altogether to defeat, these Japanese moves. There seems no doubt that certain Chinese forces will come under the general command of Lord Louis Mountbatten, when the campaign gets under way.

It should not be supposed that if the Burma campaign is successful, and the famous Burma Road is reopened, the immediate result will be a great increase in the flow of outside aid into China. There will be some increase, of course; not only by the road, with its capacity of 15,000 tons a month,* but by the opening of better and shorter air routes.

The real relief of China will come only when United Nations ships can enter Chinese ports, with rail access to the interior: such ports as Hongkong and Canton. Not until then can we really begin to help China; not until then can we start building up and equipping a Chinese army; not until then can we start large-scale air attacks against Japan from Chinese bases.

But the moral effect of the reopening of the Burma Road will be very great. It will be a boost to the spirits of every Chinese. And the material results are not to be despised, small as they may be; for if they are wisely used, they will serve to

* According to Chinese estimates in 1941.

build up the fighting power of the American 14th Air Force, now operating in China under Major General Chennault, and of the Chinese Air Force which is working in conjunction with Chennault's squadrons. These air elements, if they could be reinforced and if they can be continuously employed (instead of, as at present, having painfully to accumulate fuel and bombs over long periods in order to make brief spasmodic efforts at considerable intervals of time) can not only give the Chinese armies invaluable support against the Japanese, but they can also begin to be a real threat to Japanese shipping in the Strait of Formosa and to Japanese depots and centers of activity around the mouth of the Yangtze River, in the vicinity of Canton and in Indo-China.

Attacks on shipping are of especial importance; probably it would be better to concentrate at first on medium bombers for this purpose, rather than 4-engine bombers for long range forays against Japan itself, as far as air bases in China are concerned. The Japanese have suffered heavy losses in their steel, ocean-going steam merchant fleet. They cannot replace these losses as rapidly as they occur; they are therefore supplementing their lagging shipbuilding program in various ways—by stopping the manufacture of tanks and armored cars and devoting the steel to ships and planes, for example. But mainly, they are turning to dependence on wooden ships. For these, the material and to some extent the necessary skills are available not only in Japan, but in the Chinese ports held by the Japanese, and in Malaya, Indo-China, and the Netherlands Indies. Wooden sailing ships with small auxiliary motors, barges with motors originally designed for tanks or trucks, and barges to be towed by steam or motor tugs, are being turned out in great numbers. A coastal traffic along the Chinese coast from the Yangtze down to Canton, and thence along the coast of Indo-China down to Singapore and over to the various island groups, is taking a great part of the load off the Japanese ocean shipping. One arm of this barge traffic runs all the way out to New Guinea, skirting the northern coast of that great island.

Against Japanese ocean shipping, our most formidable weapon at present is the submarine. One of the major objects of our campaign in the Pacific is to gain submarine bases closer to the focal areas of that shipping. The curve of Japanese shipping losses will rise as our base situation improves and as the number of Allied submarines in the Far East increases, both from new construction and from transfers from the Atlantic and Mediterranean. But the submarine is not an economical or very useful weapon against small coastal vessels and barges. The airplane and the small patrol boat are their natural enemies.

If you will now turn back to the six "immediate objectives" of this preliminary period of the war against Japan, you will find that all six of them are served by an invasion of Burma. Not fully accomplished, of course; but contributed to. But Burma is only one of several areas where these objectives may be helped forward.

Next let us take the South and Southwest Pacific. Here we are now fighting to clear the Japanese out of the Solomon Islands and from the north coast of New Guinea, in preparation for a concentric attack on Rabaul, in New Britain Island, the chief Japanese base in this region. When Rabaul has been taken, there will be almost 800 miles of open water separating us from the next nearest Japanese base, which is the coral group of Truk, in the Western Carolines. Truk is at present a vitally important Japanese outpost, a base perhaps comparable in capacity and strength to our own Pearl Harbor. As long as the Japanese hold some of the Solomons and their present posts in New Britain, the Admiralty Islands and New Guinea, Truk forms the center of a vast web of island bases, of which the other sectors are the Eastern Carolines and the

Marshalls, with Wake. Guam and the Marianas and Bonins form the connecting links with Japan, and Yap and the Palaus the connecting links with the Philippines.

But if Truk loses its outposts on the south, it is then exposed to direct attack. Not only does it become a sector of the firing line, so to speak, instead of a central supporting base; but all the other outposts which were dependent upon it are fatally weakened and can hardly be supplied or reinforced at all save at prohibitive expense. Thus as we go forward to Rabaul, we not only weaken Truk, but we render almost untenable the Japanese positions in the Eastern Caroline and Marshall islands; they have already lost the Gilberts. Furthermore we move the base of our submarine activities much closer to the vital target areas south of Japan. We thus serve all but the first of our stated preliminary objectives in this move.

Next let us take the North Pacific. Here we have recovered Attu and Kiska, and thus freed the Aleutian Islands altogether of the Japanese. We can now turn to the offensive in this sector. The Japanese advance base at Paramushiru, northernmost of the Kurile Islands, is within reach. At this point the Japanese resistance must begin to be truly desperate, for if we obtain a lodgment in the Kuriles, not only can we begin air attacks against the northern part of the Japanese home islands, but also we can launch forth flotillas of patrol vessels to sweep up and destroy the Japanese fishing industry in these northern waters, thus depriving the Japanese people of a vital part of their already depleted food supply. The third, fifth and sixth of our immediate objectives are served by an advance to Paramushiru.

But now let us consider the Far Eastern theater of operations as a whole, and from the Japanese viewpoint. Suppose we succeed in retaking Burma and Rabaul and capturing the Marshall Islands and Paramushiru: surely not a tremendous series of assumptions in view of our rising power relatively to

Japan's. Suppose the Japanese must choose, then, between preventing us from marching down the long line of the Kuriles, one by one, toward their main northern island of Hokkaido, or defending Truk—we may well assume that they have not the forces to do both, especially air and naval forces. Under those conditions, they are compelled to give up Truk. By doing that, they expose Guam, the Palaus and the Philippines. If they lose Guam and the Palaus, their southern sea lanes are almost wholly severed; if they lose the Philippines, they are cut off definitely and completely from South China, Indo-China, Malaya, the Netherlands Indies, Burma and Thailand. So somewhere in this process, the Japanese must in all probability choose a moment for the playing of their reserve card—their battle fleet.

They do not want to play that card before the fate of Germany has been decided, and their opportunity for their great peace gesture is at hand. They want, in fact, to keep that ace in reserve as the chief support of their bargaining power at that time. We want to compel them to play it, because we believe that if they play it they will lose it; especially if we can compel them to play it under conditions of our choosing.

These are the conditions under which the war in the Pacific must be prosecuted up to the time when the defeat of Germany releases increased forces for use in the Far East. What happens after that will be an increase in the tempo of the fighting. With more power, more shipping, more transport planes, we can move more easily, more quickly, we can strike harder blows at more places, we can compel the Japanese to scatter their substance over more extended fronts, or in the alternative to give up that which they can no longer defend.

We may say, that from the strategic point of view, the second stage of the war against Japan ends when our air and sea power command the two strategic triangles Manila-Hong Kong-Formosa, and Shanghai-Formosa-Amamioshima. When this has happened, Japan will be cut off from all her southern conquests, in which remaining Japanese garrisons can thereafter be mopped up. She will be unable to draw supplies from the Asiatic continent save by routes entirely within the Sea of Japan, which is in effect a Japanese lake (with the exception of the Russian ports) and of which Japan commands all four of the very narrow entrances. The strain thus put on the railways of Korea will be very great, and it should not be impossible to organize sabotage against them. The Japanese supplies of cereals, iron and coal will have to be further rationed at a time when the Japanese fishing fleet will probably have ceased to exist.

Meanwhile, China will have begun her recovery.

The moment the great seaports of South China are open to us, supplies of all sorts will pour in for the Chinese armies and people. Backed by an overwhelming Allied air power, the Chinese will certainly drive the Japanese not only out of Hankow and Nanking and Shanghai, but out of all North China as well. The Japanese may, however, be able to make a stout defense of Manchukuo, because of the difficulty of the approaches from the Chinese side. That, and much else, will depend largely on the attitude of the Russians.

Indeed, at this stage, it will be for the Russians to say whether the final reduction of Japan shall involve a long war or a short war. The Russians have the advantage of position. If they launch their veteran armies into Manchuria and Korea, it will not be the thirty-odd Japanese divisions now holding that bleak frontier which will withstand them. If they open their big Maritime Province air bases to our long-range bombers, supplemented by their own, the Japanese "heartland," the island of Honshu with all its industries and teeming cities, will feel such blows as Japan has never felt before. If they send out their submarines from Vladivostok, then for the first time the Japanaese communications with the Asiatic mainland across the Sea of Japan will be endangered. There might be stern fighting, but in the end the Allied forces would inevitably occupy the whole of the coasts opposite Japan, with complete air and naval superiority—and the launching of a successful and decisive invasion would then be possible in numbers truly overwhelming.

Without the Russians, the task would be more difficult, more costly, and more lengthy. We would then have to fight hard to obtain bases from which the Japanese vital centers could be really heavily bombed. Probably we could do this at the least cost by landing in Hokkaido; but if this proved too difficult, we might have to smash our way through the mountain gates of Manchukuo and so into Korea. An invasion of Japan proper might even then be far off, until the effect of starvation had been felt. It might be a case of the Japanese yielding to bombing and blockade rather than to direct assault—for it is always possible that the fanatical fighting spirit of the individual Japanese may disappear when he is face to face with the unmistakable fact of defeat, when he finds the whole moral and spiritual structure of his life's faith crumbling into dust beneath his feet.

As we press on to the decisive blows against Japan's heart, we shall leave behind us many a difficult little problem. We shall, first of all, leave behind numerous small pockets of Japanese resistance, scattered through the Indo-Chinese peninsula, in China itself, and in various island strongholds. These Japanese we shall not at first have time to mop up; in many cases to do so would fatally delay our major operations. They must be left to be dealt with by local forces. In China, the Burmese hill states, the Philippines and probably in Celebes, we need have no anxiety about raising levies for such purposes from the population, with proper equipment and small supporting detachments of trained troops.

But in most of Burma, Thailand, Malaya, most of the Netherlands Indies and French Indo-China, we cannot in all probability have the same degree of dependence in locally raised forces, nor in the general support of the people.

It is in these areas that the Japanese have had the most success in "selling" their Greater East Asia Co-Prosperity ideas, and they have based all their efforts on good treatment for the inhabitants and the maintenance of the strictest discipline and accountability for the forces of occupation. Many natives of these parts were only too happy to see the white man thrown out by a colored race, and the Japanese have seen to it that they did not immediately find themselves under a far more grinding tyranny. That, in the Japanese view, can come later on if necessary. For the moment, the Japanese idea is to make —if not allies—at least not unwilling cooperators out of all these millions of folk. It is the Japanaese moment for the velvet glove, without too much suggestion of the iron hand within, and they have been astute enough to see it. The last thing they desire is to get these people into a frame of mind where they would welcome American and British landing forces or paratroopers with open arms and beg only to be given a gun with which to go hunt Japs.

Of course the Japanese haven't had complete success everywhere with this program of sweetness and light. In the Philippines it has been a flat failure except for a handful of scurvy politicians and time-servers, because to the average Filipino with his comparatively high standard of living, "co-prosperity" just means that he sinks to the economic level of the Javanese or the Malay, whom he despises. That is one reason why the Philippines form a natural military objective for our amphibious power; once we get in there, we shall have a strong tough native army to fight at our side. There are tough martial races also in the Celebes, and in the hill country of Burma and Indo-China, who can be counted on to some extent. But when all that is said, we are still faced with the problem of dealing with some hundred and thirty million people of varying race and religion, scattered from the borders of India to the Strait of Formosa and the eastern end of New Guinea, with pockets of Japanese fighters pock-marking the whole area.

Complicating this problem, unless there is previous agreement on the subject, will be the moves of the British, the French and the Dutch to reclaim all of their respective former authority and possessions; there will also be native rulers such as the Kings of Annam and Cambodia and the Javanese and Malay sultans to be dealt with; and there will be any number of nationalist societies and cliques which will spring to light, some violently and some peacefully, demanding each its little place in the sun of our victory. Thailand will present a special problem all its own. The Chinese will want Formosa returned to them, and not inconceivably (nor wholly illogically) may present a claim to the former Chinese holdings in Tonkin and Annam, through which a weak French regime allowed the Japanese to stab China in the back.

The possible complications are endless—to say nothing of the complications which might arise in Manchukuo if the Chinese decided they didn't want the Russians to come in, or if the Russians being in, decided they didn't want to get out. To this we might add the difficulties to be expected from the Chinese Communist forces, whose future attitude and objectives may well be considered uncertain.

It may perhaps be necessary to use Indian, Chinese and possibly Filipino troops to mop up the Japanese in most of the region under discussion. At the very best the British and American troops which can be sent to the Far East, after allowing for the maintenance of order in Europe, the police of disturbed areas, the occupation and disarmament of Germany and the guarding of the lines of communication, cannot be more than enough for the direct blows that must be rained upon the Japanese central forces.

And we must further face the fact that we do not know what the Japanese will leave behind them when they are driven out of some of these places. The policy of sweetness and light may then undergo a change. The bitterness of defeat in Japanese hearts may be cruelly visited upon the helpless people within their power.

Finally, even when Japan is beaten, we cannot foresee what the conditions in Japan itself may be. Possibly utter chaos, due to the collapse of confidence in authority; possibly a vengeful turning upon the Army and the national leaders by the masses of deluded folk whose sacrifices have been in vain —possibly, on the other hand, fatalistic submission to the decrees of an inexorable Fate, and resistance to the bitter end.

This much is clear—the political problems to be faced in the reconquest of East Asia and the smashing of the military power of Japan are no less formidable, may be more so, than those which are to be faced in the rescue of Europe from the German grip. The solution of these problems is impossible without unity of policy among the victorious powers; and that unity must be attained now, for many of these problems cannot wait for the end of the war, but must be faced and solved, at least in their preliminary stages, during the progress of military operations which may be of considerable duration.

When Japan is finally broken, what conditions shall we find in the Far East in general?

We shall have there the same sort of combined Allied commands that will exist in Europe when Germany is defeated, save that these commands will be even more diversified in character. It is quite possible that in the decisive theater we shall have Chinese armies and air forces, British, American and Russian armies, air forces and fleets (with the British including strong Dominion and Indian contingents), and perhaps French, Filipino and Dutch units of various sorts.

Scattered all through the areas from which the Japanese

have been driven will be little centers where Japanese detachments are still holding out, or have recently been mopped up. The government of the Philippine Commonwealth will probably be operating, and we may hope that some sort of stable government will be taking hold in China despite the Communist complication; but what sort of provisional or other government there will be in the rest of the area in question no one can now foresee.

With the coming of peace, every nation concerned will immediately be face to face with a series of very difficult situations. The British, for example, will have renewed problems to face in India, the Chinese will have Manchuria and Mongolia to think of, the future of Korea will have to be determined, and in all East Asia there will be the task of getting people back to work, of replacing the war structure with the peace structure, of demobilizing the enormous establishments of the lines of communication by which Japan has been defeated, and the replacement of Japanese authority with some other acceptable authority which can in each community concerned begin to deal with affairs affecting the public welfare.

I do not pretend to be able to present solutions for all these problems. Many of them will not be wholly solved for many years, if at all. But it is abundantly clear that unless there is previous discussion of them by all concerned, and some degree of unity upon the broad general principles which must govern their solution, they contain the possibilities of endless friction and difficulty among the United Nations. It is further clear that these possibilities will only be accentuated if, in the policies agreed upon, the only viewpoints receiving attention are those of Washington, London, Moscow and Chungking, without due consideration for the wishes, the feelings and the aspirations of the millions of people who live in the territories affected.

Nor will it suffice merely to lay down general principles.

The application of these principles to conditions which cannot ever be wholly foreseen, involves the need for an agency possessing the necessary authority to act, and the organization to enable it to act efficiently without loss of time, without allowing events to overtake it and confront it with accomplished facts while governments and legislatures engage in endless and distant debate.

The military agencies for the preservation of general order, the disarmament of Japan and the temporary administration of enemy territory will be on the ground, and will possess a high degree of coordination. This will necessarily be true. It is an essential ingredient of victory. But with the end of the war begins immediately the dissolution of these military forces. There must be a political agency which can supervise that task, which can carry the principle of Allied unity into the post-war period and which can serve the interests of all the Allied powers and of humanity in general, in binding up the wounds of the war, in caring for its casualties, and in making the transition from the conditions of war to those of peace. The military forces are in every sense but the tools of the civil authority. The tools will be ready, but there must be firm hands to grasp and use them.

8. THE PERIOD OF DEMOBILIZATION

THE ORGANIZATION of the whole power and resources of a nation for the fighting of total war is a tremendous task. It means that every other objective and every other interest must give way to the single purpose of obtaining victory over the enemy in the shortest possible time. The extent to which this affects the normal lives and fortunes of the people as a whole, and of each individual among them, varies somewhat, but is in sum total enormous and is inescapable as to any person or family.

It is hardly necessary to describe this process in detail. We are going through it now, and we all understand pretty well what it means, and how it has affected each of us. We have yet to see how the reverse of this process, the process of demobilization, may affect us. It does not lie within the province of this book to examine what the economic processes or results of demobilization may be. It is, I think, self-evident that it must be as carefully planned as the mobilization of our resources for war. It must proceed by stages, as the resumed activities of peace show themselves able to absorb the temporarily diverted resources of the state in man-power, material and productive capacity. We are here concerned with the effect of that process, in the United States and elsewhere, on the international structure and on the prospects of maintaining throughout the world a reasonable degree of peace and order.

Demobilization in this war will probably have two phases;

that which follows the defeat of Germany, and that which follows the defeat of Japan.

We have already examined the dangers which may attend the defeat of Germany, if that event is immediately followed by a Japanese peace offer. It would be a mistake to add to the psychological effect of Germany's downfall, a great relaxation of the war-time measures and regulations which control our internal war effort, or to permit the demobilization of our armed forces in too considerable a degree. There will be great pressure to bring home and disband "useless" troops, and there will be offered in the press and over the radio a great deal of volunteer advice as to just how many troops we can "get along with" in the war against Japan. We shall be told in great detail how that war ought to be finished by our Navy and air force, using Chinese and Indian man-power for ground forces. Every family with a boy overseas will be made to feel that it has a right to have that particular boy brought home at once; every business which is suffering war-time restrictions will clamor for the relaxing of those restrictions as no longer essential to a "much reduced" war effort.

But actually, as we have tried to show, the war against Japan will be no simple or easy war; and the greater the force we throw into it, the quicker it will be over. Even if we are to assume that air power and sea blockade will be its controlling factors, and may actually prove to be the decisive factors, there will still be heavy land fighting to be undertaken in order to gain possession of the necessary bases for our air and naval forces, and to deprive the Japanese of the resources of any part of the Asiatic continent. We may believe that the Russians will be ready to aid us, but it will not be quickly or easily that the Russians can turn from Europe to Asia, and begin to develop anything like their full strength far out at the eastern end of their trans-Siberian rail lines. As for the Chinese, they have men but they do not have modern weapons or equipment;

they will need vast supplies and a long period of training. There will be plenty for British and American troops to do in the Far East.

The controlling factor is really the factor of shipping. There is a limit to the number of troops that can be maintained, from European and American bases, in any part of East Asia. And there are certain deductions that must be made from the available shipping before we can begin to count our possible development of fighting power in the East.

Probably the first claim on the available shipping will be for the relief of the starving and destitute populations of a great part of liberated Europe. The people of the British Isles must continue to be fed. The minimum trade requirements of Latin America must be met. The supply of the Allied forces in Europe must continue to be assured. When these and other claims have been balanced against the needs of the Far East, it may be possible to determine the size of the forces which can be sent there, and maintained there; and to bring this into accord with the plans for the prosecution of the war against Japan.

There will remain a certain residue of American and British man-power in Europe which can be sent home. It will be better to do this by establishing certain classifications of individuals, than by selecting units arbitrarily for demobilization. Physical condition, family requirements, and the need of home industry for men of particular skills should be taken into account. The number and type of units required (a) for the temporary police of Germany and its satellites; (b) for the campaign in the Far East; and (c) for the security of lines of communication, should be determined, and units selected for these duties should be cleared of men of the categories determined on for demobilization, vacancies being filled by transfers from other units, including volunteers. This will of course result in considerable confusion unless very carefully planned in advance, and unless it proceeds on the basis of a plan which has the full approval of all the powers involved.

In any case it will not be accomplished quickly. It will be a gradual process, and many units may have to be sent to the Far East without having been, so to speak, weeded out.

At the same time, there will be going on throughout Europe the process of establishing law and order, the organization of governments, and the taking over by local authorities of the duties of police and relief. The withdrawal of Allied troops should keep pace with this process so far as possible. There will be innumerable complications. For example: Poland lies between Russia and Germany. There will doubtless be a considerable Russian army of occupation in Germany, whose lines of communication will lie through Poland. It will be only natural that the Russian military authorities will desire to maintain the control of these lines of communication, and it will be only natural that the Poles will demand the evacuation of their territory by Russian troops at the earliest possible moment. The only way that clashes can be prevented is by a previous and proclaimed agreement among the great powers as to the terms and conditions of demobilization, disarmament and police. Then the temporary presence of Russian troops in Poland, if necessary, should be recognized by the Poles as a measure taken in the common interest and not as a unilateral Russian procedure, and the Russians, for their part, should understand that they are acting not primarily as Russians, but as agents of the Council of the United Nations. It is one thing for the ancient doctrine of "military necessity" to be interpreted by a single government on the advice of its own general staff; it is quite another for that doctrine and its implications to be applied in particular cases by an international authority which takes into account not only immediate military considerations but is basically guided by the common need for restoring as soon as possible the general peace and well-being of Europe.

As we look forward to this point we begin to see how vitally important it is that the beginnings of the United Nations Council should be made now, so that the Council may have acquired experience and authority by the time it really begins to need them. If we have to end the war first, and begin our political organization afterward, the results can never be wholly satisfactory. We shall be trying to build a cooperative political structure in an atmosphere in which all sorts of disruptive forces—now restrained, modified or held inoperative by the fact of war and the existence of a still dangerous enemy—will have been released.

One of the greatest tasks to be undertaken in Europe during the period of demobilization will be the establishment of reliable systems of transport and communications. Transport will be needed for the movement of food and relief supplies to the areas where they are required; for the return of refugees to their homes; for the evacuation to hospitalization centers of sick and wounded; for troop movements; and beside all these emergency measures, for the normal returning needs of European life. The railways of Europe will be quite unable to bear the strain, after years of war in which the Germans will have stripped some nations of locomotives and rolling stock for their own use, in which railway establishments of every sort have been the target for bombs, shells and guerrilla activities, and in which the proper maintenance either of equipment or right-of-way has been progressively more difficult. It will be necessary to organize, until the railways can be restored, a huge system of motor-transport, both for freight and passengers, to be equipped from the vast motor-transport pools of the Allied armies, and operated as far as possible on regular schedules over established routes. This system should be supplemented by rail transport where possible, and by the local bus and trucking services which communities normally maintain. It should be further supplemented by the rapid development of a system of air transportation, in which there should be no hesitation in using military planes at first, when planes of commercial or transport types are not available.

Side by side with this must come a system of communications, using radio as its basis, with the restoration of telegraph and telephone lines, and local telephone systems, as rapidly as conditions permit. The mail can be carried by special units of the motor-transport service where necessary, and it will of course be the responsibility of each country to restore its postal service to a working basis as quickly as it can. Until this can be done, mail will have to be handled under international authority.

The United Nations Council will almost certainly find itself obliged to set up a European Transport Authority and a European Communications Authority, to administer these two systems. At first the operating personnel and control may have to be military; civilian personnel and civilian control should be introduced as rapidly as possible. The guiding principle should be to get goods and people moving in the right directions, to reestablish communications, and so to contribute as quickly and efficiently as possible to the restoration of normal life throughout the continent. This can only be done by a centralized authority which has the power to act, which can prevent the setting up (during the transition period) of troublesome police and customs barriers, and which is operated for the greatest good of the greatest number of people.

All this is not to say it should be the task of the United Nations Council to try to realize at one bound, and by means of its temporary military control, a United States of Europe. But it is essential that the Council should act effectively, and with the means it has at hand, to preserve as much of the human and the material foundations for a new Europe as it can; that is its plain duty. If the peoples of Europe find the work of the Council worth preserving, as they gradually reassume the attributes of sovereignty, that will be the most worthwhile testimony possible of the value of what has been done.

It is of course to be understood, that as fast as stable governments are organized in the various countries of Europe which are now under German occupation, those governments will assume local control. It should be within the powers of the Council to extend temporary recognition to such governments within defined boundaries, without prejudice to whatever final settlement may be reached as to permanent boundaries when the time comes for translating the work of the demobilization period into a permanent political structure for Europe.

With the immense task to be accomplished by the United Nations Relief and Rehabilitation Administration, we cannot here deal in detail. It is obvious that the work of this organization will be immensely facilitated if it is brought within the scope of a political authority which can coordinate the policies of the several governments concerned, and if—through the overall supervision of such a political agency—it is enabled to work in complete harmony with the agencies having to do with transport and communications.

It is likewise obvious that none of these various agencies can do their work properly, unless they are operating under conditions which insure the maintenance of public order. That, indeed, should be the most important test of the right to recognition of any temporary government: that it commands the allegiance of the population to a sufficient degree that it can maintain order, domestic peace, without resort to extraordinary methods of suppression. It may well turn out that some of the existing governments-in-exile may not be well received, or indeed received at all, by the peoples of the countries to which they respectively appertain. The Council may be confronted by governments which spring to life from underground movements, and which will command popular support as against the presently recognized government-in-exile. The Council may likewise be confronted by local conditions tantamount to civil war, arising from the claims of rival candidates or parties. In these disputes, it would be fatal to the authority of the Council for it to take sides. It must maintain the security of lines of transport and communication. It must ensure the equitable distribution of relief. To that extent, and it is a considerable extent, it must maintain public order wherever that task cannot be locally performed, and until at least provisional recognition has been given to a local government. It must be prepared even to withdraw such recognition in extreme cases where it has become apparent that the local government cannot discharge its responsibilities. But it must be made plain to all concerned that the authority and actions of the Council in such matters are but temporary expedients, and that under no circumstances is there any intention on the part of the great military powers to dictate either the form or the composition of the government of any people in Europe.

It is within these limitations, and in this spirit, that a Council of the United Nations can proceed, when Germany has been finally defeated and occupied, to take preliminary and provisional action for re-establishing peace and order in Europe. The force behind the Council's measures, will in great part be provided by the United States, Great Britain and Russia. It seems likely that the French will be able to aid to some degree from the beginning, since a condition precedent to the reduction of Germany to impotence is probably an Allied invasion of France, which will automatically bring about the re-establishment of a French popular government on French soil. It seems likely, also, that as soon as there is a foothold for them, there will be stable Dutch, Norwegian and Danish governments, though these cannot contribute greatly to the police of German and satellite territory. The immediate future of the other occupied nations is less certain.

But the force, the miltary force which must stand back of these provisional arrangements until Europe can be reestablished on a basis of recognized law, must be largely American, British and Russian.

The various units of the armies, air forces and navies of these countries which are assigned for this purpose will, in effect, constitute an international police force. They will be under the command of officers experienced in the command of mixed international forces, and they will be operated and administered by mixed staffs accustomed to working together. The numbers of troops, ships and planes actually assigned to various tasks will be reduced as circumstances permit; and gradually volunteers will take the place of men enlisted under draft laws for war service, at least in the American and British contingents. Of course, while this process is going on, the constituted authorities of each nation will be considering the needs of each country for a permanent military establishment. They will, it is to be hoped, take into account the uses to which that establishment is to be put, and they will have before them, as an actual demonstration of such uses, the *de facto* accomplishments of the United Nations Council in laying the foundation for a new Europe.

It may be added, that the United Nations Council will possess in the control of relief and rehabilitation, transport and communications, a sum total of influence which should go far to enable it to maintain order and ensure the peaceful settlement of local troubles without having recourse to the use of force. The existence of adequate force will be necessary and salutary; but, existing, it may not have to be used in the majority of cases.

As to the financing of these various services, of course the powers maintaining any measure of military force in Europe will bear the charges for their own forces. In the beginning, the victorious powers will probably have to bear the charges of the other services as well; but these should be, and must be transferred in due proportion to the budgets of the nations which benefit from them, in such degree as may be possible and as quickly as conditions permit. Nothing could be more potentially dangerous to the future of international cooperation in the world, than to have the American people, or the British people, or any other, convinced that they were being made to bear an unfair share of such costs, or that they were to be the permanent underwriters of the economy of Europe.

So far, we have considered some of the questions which will claim attention in Europe when Germany is beaten. There is no pretense that this is an exhaustive survey of the situation. The points which it is hoped have been established beyond question are these: (1) that order must be maintained, temporarily, by those who have the power to do it, that is, the victors in this war; and (2) that these victors must possess a political agency for exercising that power, so that they may act in unity and not at cross purposes.

The same problems, differing in detail and degree, will arise in East Asia when Japan has been defeated. Measures similar in principle will have to be taken to deal with them. In East Asia, however, one of the United Nations, China, is by far the largest and most important nation, and it is in adjusting the relations of the other United Nations with China that the solution of the most immediately important problems of the demobilization period must be sought. Complete candor compels the admission that this will not be as easy as it sounds. Within the territory which properly belongs to China, there are elements—of which the Chinese Communists are but one, though perhaps the most numerous—which are antagonistic to the present government at Chungking. In aiding that government to expel the Japanese, the other United Nations can hardly avoid aiding it to repress its own dissidents. They may not intend to do so, but since China is a sovereign nation it is difficult for the United States, for example, to make certain that an American plane turned over to the Chinese air force to bomb the Japanese is not actually used to bomb a peasant uprising in Kansu. In this fact lie the seeds of future trouble. But it is all the more necessary that there should be a political agency in which those seeds can be dealt with, and prevented from sprouting into noxious weeds.

Transport in East Asia will be largely a matter of shipping, and of the rehabilitation of Chinese roads and railways. Both transport and communications will represent a more difficult problem than in Europe, because the original systems are not so extensive. Special thought may have to be given to Chinese river transport, as well as to river shipping in Indo-China and Burma. Each country, and each people concerned will represent a separate and special problem. The maintenance of order will require forces of ground troops or special constabulary, for which local manpower may be drawn upon in many instances. It hardly seems likely, however, that it will be either necessary or indeed desirable to maintain the forces of other United Nations on Chinese soil for any length of time after the Japanese have been finally compelled to submit, save perhaps by special arrangement in the case of a few temporary air bases for keeping watch and ward over Japan until the police of the Far East can be established on a permanent basis.

In fact, there seems every prospect that with the exception of certain forces of occupation in the Japanese islands themselves, the bulk of the British and American ground forces in the Far East can be withdrawn for demobilization within a comparatively short time after the defeat of Japan and the disarmament of that country have been accomplished.

But it must be recognized, that both as to Germany and Japan, one absolutely essential preliminary to the demobilization of the United Nations forces, and in due time to the termination of the United Nations occupation of German and Japanese territory, is the disarmament of these two criminal powers.

They cannot be left in possession of the means to attempt a war of revenge, insofar as we can deprive them of such means; yet the task of disarming a great industrial state is not a simple one, nor can it be done with military considerations alone in mind. Every government concerned will be under the strongest of pressures to bring the young men home, to lift war-time restrictions on civilian economy, to let its people turn to the tasks and the pleasures and the hopes of peace. This must be done and cannot be long delayed, yet it must somehow be accomplished while at the same time providing against the recurrence of the danger which we have armed and joined together to destroy.

9. THE DISARMAMENT OF THE ENEMY POWERS

DISARMAMENT, as between sovereign states, occurs in one of three ways: (1) by mutual agreement, to obtain relief from the burdens of maintaining armed forces, and to lessen the anxieties that may lead to war; (2) by force, as imposed upon a defeated state by the victor; and (3) voluntarily, as when a State either wholly neglects its defenses, or considers (as with Denmark recently) that to maintain them can serve no purpose because the State is in any case too weak to resist more powerful neighbors.

It may be instructive to take note of the relation between disarmament and the maintenance of domestic peace within a law abiding community. Here disarmament is a matter of law. Our constitution protects the rights of citizens "to keep and bear arms," but legal interpretations of this provision have made it clear that the private citizen does not thereby escape the laws of States and lesser communities, which forbid the possession of weapons which can be concealed about the person, or of automatic weapons such as machine-guns.

What we may call the community disarmament policy does not seek to deprive the law-abiding citizen of the means of self defense in circumstances where he may need them; he can always, on proving his need and his trustworthiness, obtain permission to possess and carry weapons. On the other hand, the mere possession of weapons by a person with a criminal record is in many communities itself a punishable offense. Usually the law provides for the numbering and registration of firearms, so that their purchasers may be known to the authorities, and so that any weapon which is illegally used may be traced to its owner. The manufacture and sale of firearms are hedged round with regulations, especially applying to weapons of the more dangerous types. A criminal gang, with plenty of money to spend, may obtain a machine gun through devious illegal channels, but it is difficult for the ordinary individual criminal to get hold of such a weapon. Science has provided means by which a bullet fired from any rifled weapon may be identified with the barrel from which it was discharged. And while all these precautions are taken to deprive the criminal of weapons, or to make his use of them dangerous to himself, the armament and equipment of the police force is steadily growing more modern, more complete and more efficient in every way, placing at the disposal of the guardians of domestic peace all the resources of modern scientific and engineering progress.

Indeed, the disparity in armament as between the State and

the individual citizen has grown so great, in these days of automatic firearms, tanks, armored cars, and airplanes, that the free peoples of the world have taken the utmost precaution in their fundamental laws to protect themselves from armed tyranny by placing the most careful restrictions on the maintenance of armed forces by national or local governments. In Great Britain, for example, the authority to maintain an army is granted to the Crown by Parliament only on a single year's sufferance, the Army Act having to be renewed each year; in the United States, the size of the Army is habitually kept low by Congressional action, and the Regular Army is usually inferior in strength to the aggregate of the various forces of State militia. These are the tendencies of free peoples with regard to those military forces which they regard as necessary evils, and the same is true of police forces. No one ever heard of an American or a British community in which the executive authority considered the police budget sufficiently large; barely enough for minimum protection, and not a man more, is the usual allowance of the legislative authority which controls the public purse.

When it comes to disarmament and police in the international field, we have less experience to guide us. Disarmament by agreement was tried during the tragic twenty years which followed 1918. It was partially successful in the matter of naval disarmament, but even there it failed in the end, partly because the United States, and to some extent Great Britain, tried to combine it with voluntary disarmament—"disarmament by example"—and so failed to build even those quotas of ships which were allowed them, but more because the Japanese never regarded it as anything other than an instrument to serve their ends and discarded it the moment it ceased to be useful to them, while the Germans did exactly as they pleased as soon as the accession of Hitler gave them a chance to throw off the restraints of the Treaty of Versailles. In no other field than naval was any agreement as to mutual disarmament ever carried through, even in conference form, though the attempt was made. Mutual jealousies and suspicions, and a very real fear of the outbreak of a new war, blasted any hope of success.

Disarmament imposed upon a defeated state by force has been tried in the past, but has rarely been successful, as with Napoleon's abortive attempt to limit the size of the Prussian army. The most recent instance, and the one to which the cynics always refer in saying "It cannot be done" is the attempt to limit the armaments of Germany and her associates after the war of 1914-1918. It failed, of course, because those who imposed that disarmament upon Germany did not thereafter remain combined to enforce its continuance. They lacked any real unity of purpose. They had no common policy which was proof against even minor differences and jealousies. They cherished illusions of permanent security against Germany. And so the French and the British and their satellites quarreled among themselves, the Italians slipped away from them, the Americans stood aside, the Russians played their own single-handed game—and the Germans rearmed.

Lacking unity of purpose and effort, backed by unity of self-interest, among those to whose interest it is to preserve the peace, so will it always be. It is in such conditions of chaos and weakness that crime always flourishes—and sometimes conquers.

Actually, the disarmament of Germany was in itself quite successfully carried out at first. The Germans were deprived of their air force and their submarines; their surface fleet was reduced to a very few ships of limited fighting qualities; their army was likewise both limited in size, and fixed as to armament and organization by specific regulations. Had those limitations been maintained, Germany would have been as helpless to disturb the peace of the world as Sweden or Bulgaria. Germany became a threat to that peace only when the Germans took the first steps toward violation of their treaty obligations, and were allowed to do so with impunity. Instantly they proceeded to fresh and greater violations, as might have been expected, until at last the world awoke too late to the folly of such weakness and lack of unity. Even so, it took the Germans six solid years of intensive preparation, on top of the furtive preparation that had preceded the accession of Hitler, before they were ready to fight. They could not have done it so quickly, had they not been under complete totalitarian control, and had the resources of all the world not been freely open to them to draw upon as they liked. Probably they could not have done it even under those conditions, if the attention of the other states had not in part been distracted by the antics of Mussolini, the savage onslaught of Japan upon China, the Spanish Civil War and the aftermath of the great depression.

The building up of a great war machine from next to nothing is no easy or simple task. It is on that fact that our hopes for the future must be founded.

What measures shall we take to disarm Germany again, when this time she is again defeated? First of all, of course, will come the military measures: the laying down or handing over of arms which will be required by the Allied Commander in Chief when Germany surrenders or when her territory is fully occupied. The vessels of the German fleet will this time come into our possession either through their destruction at sea, or their surrender, or their seizure in their bases. Similarly allied forces will hold every German air field and aircraft factory. For the moment, Germany will be helpless—because she will be utterly in our power and at our mercy.

But what then? We cannot continually remain in occupation of German territory. Sooner or later, we will withdraw, and leave what remains of the German people to work out their own destiny. It is not within the realm of practical reality to suppose that the American, British, and Russian peoples will continue forever to keep a million or two million of their young men engaged in no more profitable occupation than standing guard over the Germans. Moreover, from the point of view of economic necessity, a prosperous and busy Germany is essential to a prosperous Europe. The industrial output of the United States and Great Britain combined, after taking into account the Oriental and African and Latin American markets, is unequal to meeting the tremendous demands for manufactured products that will arise as Europe seeks to rebuild its shattered civilization; nor can it be expected for many years that Russian industry will have heavy export surpluses.

But if this is so, how is Germany to be prevented from rearming?

We may begin by considering what will immediately follow the complete surrender of Germany and the complete occupation of German territory. We must presume that this will be accomplished under a general political agreement among the United Nations, for in the absence of such an agreement there will be no possibility of any orderly procedure, but rather the certainty of the return of all the ancient evils that have ever plagued alliances in their hours of triumph.

Let us proceed upon the happier supposition that some degree of unity of policy has been achieved, and that there is in existence a United Nations Council as the symbol and instrument of that unity. Germany having been defeated and occupied, we begin with an ocular and unmistakable demonstration which every German, old and young, can see with his own eyes, that Germany has been beaten by force of arms by the very nations which his leaders have taught him to despise. That will count for a good deal. It will be the beginning at least of the demonstration that crime does not pay. But it will be far from enough in itself. Many a criminal, caught, convicted, and standing before the judge for sentence, would in that moment admit his conversion to the view that crime does not pay, and feel it too; rare indeed is the criminal who in such a case will not deafen the ears of judge and probation officers and soft-hearted citizens with promises of reform. Occasionally, if he is intelligent, he will carry out those promises if given the chance; much more often, if let off lightly, he will behave himself for a little while, and then begin to think himself very smart at having so fooled the officers of justice, until presently he is back at his old tricks again. We cannot afford to take any chances on German promises, even though they may be proffered by a seemingly democratic and repentant German government such as that of the Weimar Republic.

Nevertheless, the foundation for improvement must begin with the demonstration that crime does not pay: the occupation of all Germany by the victorious armies. The German people may think themselves fortunate indeed if that demonstration is not reinforced by the massacre of thousands of their fellow countrymen by those neighbors they have misused. Certainly, as to individual German criminals, it will be reinforced by punishment at the hands of Allied justice.

About this, there must be no nonsense, no legal quibbling and no mawkish sentimentality. The men who planned and carried out this crime against all humanity must be dealt with as they deserve. It has been urged that there exists no German law under which they can be tried, and that many of them are not amenable to the ordinary municipal law of any of the Allied powers. This is true, strictly speaking; but it is precisely for such purposes that we require a United Nations Council. The United Nations should each, by appropriate legislation, empower the Council to execute justice upon such individuals as may fall within the category of international criminals, which can be a category clearly defined as including certain persons specified by name and others who have aided and abetted them or who have been guilty of inhuman outrages upon helpless civilians or prisoners of war. A special High

Court of Justice can then be established, its rules of procedure agreed upon, and the road from its bar to the gallows made a short and swift one. Of course, those individual criminals whose offenses have been committed wholly against people of a single one of the United Nations, may be turned over to the courts of that nation to be dealt with, as suggested in the Moscow Pact.

No nonsense about neutral states giving asylum to these war criminals should be tolerated for a moment. Neutrality of that sort will be non-existent in the new world community, will be as unthinkable as it would be for a private citizen to give refuge in his home to a pursued malefactor and deny admittance to a policeman with a warrant. No better opportunity for demonstrating this change could be found than by firmly refusing to recognize the right of asylum for these people in case any neutral state is so ill-advised as to admit them within its borders; and there should be no hesitation whatever in applying the irresistible pressure of economic sanctions, including complete blockade, to any state which refuses to hand over an international criminal on demand.

All this will provide an additional demonstration of the fact that crime does not pay. No such fate befell the planners of Germany's last raid upon her neighbors. No such memories arose to haunt Adolf Hitler and his henchmen as they began to plan their new series of crimes; nor their Prussian military accomplices either.

Care should be taken, in all this, to avoid acting in a spirit of indiscriminate vengeance. The legacy of hatred which that sort of thing leaves behind is one which sometimes endures for generations. No accused should be denied a fair trial in open court, with counsel to represent him, the right to call witnesses in his behalf and the right to face his accusers in the presence of his judges. There should be no star chamber proceedings, no secret sessions, no Gestapo methods. Nor should there be any tedious delays, any complicated procedures, or anything except calm, impersonal, inexorable administration of justice.

Likewise we should avoid such acts as the continuance of the blockade after the last war, which caused the deaths of so many German children. The German people should be considered as entitled, in the name of humanity, to the benefits of the United Nations relief agencies until they can take care of themselves.

We can begin, then, with a Germany in which no legend of betrayal can grow up, no legend of the invincible army which was double-crossed from within; rather, we shall have a Germany utterly broken and defeated, whose criminal leaders have been dealt with by the justice of outraged humanity, but whose children have been fed by the mercy of that same humanity. Surely this is a different soil in which to sow the seed of peace, than that of 1919-1920.

But it is only a beginning. There will still be those, when the High Court has done its work, who will retain the determination to try again. There will still be German militarists, and German professors, and German politicians, who will think of the future only in terms of Deutschland über Alles. They may have no receptive audience for their ideas in that hour of defeat and they will not expect one; they will wait for the return of prosperity, and for the day when we have forgotten and a generation which knew not Joseph is come to power in London and Washington and Moscow. Then they will hope to begin again, a little at a time, as Hitler began.

They must be deprived of the means to do so. But how?

The difficulty lies, not with the Germans but with ourselves. We know the Germans now for what they are; we know that they may again become the instruments of leaders produced from among themselves, men who cannot understand any world in which Germans are not masters and other folk slaves. But we cannot be sure that we shall continue to make even the small sacrifices which are necessary to keep Germany disarmed. We know well that we are a sentimental people, always willing to believe the best of others and easily appealed to on the ground of sympathy and compassion; we Americans know that our British associates are like us in these respects. Therefore when we take precautions against a resurgence of German aggression, we know that if those precautions are to be permanent, they must be simple, they must do no substantial injustice, and they must be such as shall appeal to the ordinary commonsense of all of us, now and hereafter. They must be such as we are all ready to take, and to maintain, against our own domestic evil-doers, and the need for them must be just as constantly apparent to the ordinary citizen.

This rules out such fanciful solutions of the German problem as forcibly dividing Germany up into separate states—Prussia, Bavaria, Saxony, etc. We might do this, but we would not thus reduce the sum total of German energy or resourcefulness. A week would not pass after the division had been effected, before there would be a secret society whose purpose was the reunion of Germany, and the very act of division would provide a perfectly legitimate and inspiring rallying point around which the German forces of resistance and revenge might gather.

There may possibly be something to be said for the proposal to set up a Catholic state in Central Europe, to include Austria and the Catholic portions of Germany (notably Bavaria and Rhenish Prussia). But it is apparent that this is not to be accomplished, or ought not to be accomplished, by an Allied ukase, but by political methods extending perhaps over a period of years, and working with those within the territory of the proposed state whose interest it may be to see such a state established. Thus it may well be that the inhabitants of the industrial regions along the Rhine, who have suffered so cruelly in this war, may not wish to find themselves again becoming at once the instruments and the victims of Prussian militarism. It may well be that the inhabitants of Austria may prefer to seek their destinies within the framework of such a state, which could be strong enough and therefore influential enough to maintain its rights and dignity among the nations of Europe, rather than return to the unhappy conditions of Austrian existence in the post-1918 period. This is hardly the place to elaborate upon the arguments for and against such an arrangement. Enough has been said to make the point that neither this nor any other political settlement of German affairs can be permanent or useful unless it is one in which those who are directly involved, the people who live in the affected territory, concur wholeheartedly, and in which the moving spirits are not Britons, or Russians, or Americans, but their own natural leaders. It may become the policy of the United Nations to bring about such a change, or some other change, but they will have to accomplish their ends through long-range political methods and not with a club.

Nor can we expect to undertake and carry through a policy involving the elaborate police and control of Germany by United Nations commissions as a permanent measure. Sooner or later we should be accused of maintaining an international Gestapo; there would be incidents, which would call for the use of troops or for humiliating retreat. These incidents would presently be tried in the court of public opinion in this country and in Great Britain, and would arouse sympathy for the German people. There would be those who would know how to make use of that sympathy. For what we would then be doing in Germany would be essentially foreign to our natures and ideals, so that in the end we would withdraw, and the British would withdraw, leaving the police of Germany completely to the Russians. That might well be the end of the United Nations, of the unity of purpose and effort upon which our hopes of the future rest.

What we do in the matter of disarming Germany can have permanence only if it be something which every American, and every Briton, as well as every Russian, can and will continue to support and understand and believe in. Within those limits, a very practical disarmament is still possible.

It consists simply of this:

(1) Germany shall not be permitted to manufacture aircraft of any kind, shape or form; or to possess military aircraft.

(2) Germany shall not be permitted to build or to possess vessels of war, whether submarine or surface vessels.

These things the ordinary folk of the free nations will support, because it is upon their bodies and the bodies of those near and dear to them, and upon their homes and their friends and upon the ships which link them together, that Germany has misused the aircraft and the warships which she has possessed in the past. It will be long, indeed, before those memories fade out. It will be long, indeed, before there can be found any considerable number of Englishmen, or of Americans either, who will think that it is safe to allow the German to have military aircraft or ships of war. And without aircraft or a fleet, Germany is helpless to war upon her neighbors, or to protect herself from punitive or restraining action by the United Nations should that become necessary.

No nation, under modern conditions, can go to war without an air force. It may be said, will not the Germans build up a great land army, with new and fearsome weapons of every kind, and risk the bombs while she marches upon her neighbors as of old and ravages their lands? No. For while the specific terms of German disarmament will be the deprivation of the right to manufacture aircraft and naval vessels, any attempt by the Germans to create an oversize land army, one obviously intended for aggressive purposes, cannot be concealed, and will, immediately it is perceived, become the proper object of the attention of the United Nations Council, which will make appropriate recommendations and be prepared to take appropriate action. Great armaments of any sort are not to be built up in a day; and air power, swift and hard-hitting, is the very weapon to destroy in embryo the beginnings of such dangerous re-armament, while yet they are but beginnings.

Are we, then, to deny the Germans the possession of commercial aircraft? No, not when they have set up for themselves a government which gives some promise of good purposes. That would be unfairly to restrict the reconstruction of Germany in an age which will be the great air age. But not for a long time, at any rate, may Germany manufacture such things for herself. She may buy them abroad, and use them for her commercial purposes; their type and numbers and characteristics will be limited by international agreement, their replacement will be permitted only after a due lapse of time, and they will be subject to periodic inspection by United Nations agents to see to it that they are not being adapted for military use. Under such conditions, they are as harmless as so many toys.

Will the Germans not set up a secret aircraft industry? No. There should be a thorough inspection system; and beyond that, the development of military aircraft requires research and experiment and endless test, and the testing of airplanes is something that cannot be concealed because it requires flight. Not only will German air be regularly patrolled by United Nations reconnaissance planes, but it will be constantly crossed and recrossed by the commercial planes of non-German states, whose pilots will be quick to report any unauthorized aircraft of military type which they may see. Germany will not be permitted to set aside zones in which foreign aircraft are forbidden to fly.

Will Germany not, as she did before, arrange for German pilots to be trained abroad, and for a German aircraft industry to be set up in foreign countries? No. For it will be provided, by each of the United Nations, that no German national, or former German national, can ever be employed, in any capacity whatsoever, from chief engineer to sweeper, in any aircraft plant or any other factory or commercial organization having anything to do with the manufacture, maintenance or operation of aircraft, or of engines or parts for aircraft. If any non-member state permits such a thing, that state will immediately be placed under the same restrictions as Germany, by the proper exercise of police power for the good of the world community.

Moreover, and this is of vital importance in other matters than the production of aircraft, it will be forbidden for the German government, or any German corporation, or any German national, to own either real estate, or so much as a single share of stock or a single dollar's worth of the securities of any non-German corporation or other business enterprise of any kind, shape or form whatsoever. All German transactions with the rest of the world, of financial or commercial character, should be subject to the scrutiny of a United Nations commercial agency, in order that such transactions shall be limited to the ordinary processes of commercial exchange and shall not permit of any undue German influence accruing in any non-German area.

It may well be recognized that reparations can hardly be collected from post-war Germany to anything like the extent to which German criminality has damaged the other nations of the world. The Russians have announced that they will have certain claims to present in the matter of German machine tools, precision instruments and other equipment with which to restore Russian industry that the Germans have damaged. Possibly other such reparations in kind may be required of Germany by others of the United Nations. The history of monetary reparations after the last war is not encouraging, however. Yet assuredly every care should be exercised to see to it that by no ingenious device shall Germany, or any German, profit from their buccaneering expedition. To this end, without any prolonged argument about legal points, all German holdings of any kind outside of Germany should be confiscated; and if title cannot be ascertained, the said holdings should pass to the credit of the United Nations Relief and Rehabilitation Administration.

The right of residence of German nationals outside of Germany may well be restricted, in view of the abuse to which such right of residence has been put during the past. It might very properly be decreed by the United Nations Council that Germany shall have no right to maintain consulates or commercial agencies abroad, except under such regulation as shall prevent the abuse of this privilege. The conditions under which Germany may maintain diplomatic relations with the United Nations should be the subject of careful examination, to the end that this privilege may not be abused by the Germans as it has been in recent years. If this privilege is allowed at all, it should be under strict regulation as to the number of personnel allowed in each mission, and as to the extent to which diplomatic immunities may be extended to any such personnel other than to the ambassadors or ministers themselves. All this is perfectly in accord with the customary treatment of criminals by the agencies of an organized society. It is quite well understood that the conviction of crime involves the loss of civil rights, which may be restored in whole or in part only upon clear evidence of repentance and reform.

Another step which seems advisable is the taking over, completely, of the archives of the German General Staff, which should be transferred to United Nations territory for study and safekeeping. This accumulated mass of military and political research has been many years in the building, and has been of immense benefit to the German military planners in all their wars against their neighbors. The same principle, of course, should be applied to such accumulations of records and research material as that of General Haushofer's Geopolitical Institute at Munich.

There is nothing in the conditions as stated to prevent the Germans from rebuilding their industry and their political institutions or from pursuing their own way of life as long as that does not include the invasion of the rights of their neighbors. The precautions to be taken are against German rearmament, and likewise against any possibility that Germans may derive pecuniary profit from their recent misconduct, or may in future by any device acquire undue influence outside of Germany. It must be admitted that Germans may find themselves suffering under regulations which will deprive them of a wholly equal opportunity to compete in foreign markets with other states. For this condition, they have only themselves to thank. It is probable that if there arises in Germany a generation which is content with fair and reasonable methods of competition, the artificial restrictions imposed upon a suspect Germany may gradually be relaxed. Until it is evident that such is the case, no German can be surprised or feel honest outrage at being treated with suspicion and kept under watchful surveillance in all his dealings with others.

It is of course to be recognized that there enters into all these suggestions, the factor of our own willingness to maintain the proposed restrictions. Most of them will be maintained as right and just by those who have suffered at German hands, as long as the memory of German ill-doing remains fresh. After awhile, change will certainly come. There will be all sorts of pressures tending to that end—pressures of German origin, and pressures from those who think they might profit by doing business with Germans under less strict regulation, and pressures from those among us who invariably sympathize with evil doers who have been caught and are being made to pay the penalty of their crimes: the sort of folk who send flowers to convicted murderers. Yet in sum total it may be reasonably expected that these restrictions will for a long time paralyze the German power to do evil in this world, and it may also be expected that of all the proposed restrictions, that which forbids the Germans to possess an aircraft industry, or to have a navy, will last the longest.

This being so, we may hope that in the interval of safety thus gained, the remainder of the world may perfect its organization as a community, for the preservation of peace; so that in the end, it shall be apparent even to Germans that there will be no profit in attempting to resume the criminal career from which they are now in the process of being dissuaded by great force and at ultimate sacrifice.

Indeed it may well prove that the threat of a possibly resurgent Germany, may be the cement that will hold together the fabric of the United Nations until we have become accustomed to working together and acting together—just as the threat of British vengeance held together the United States for so long after the somewhat reluctant adoption of the Constitution, and eventually ushered in the "Era of Good Feeling" which followed the close of the War of 1812.

It would, however, be unwise to put too much strain upon a new and untried structure. We shall have quite enough to do to solve the problems of relief and reconstruction that will require attention both in Europe and in Asia, while preventing the resurgence of a defeated Germany. Within Europe, we need fear no other enemy. Italy, Bulgaria, Hungary are not dangers to world peace except as they may cooperate with the Germans. By themselves they are not formidable.

Japan is a different sort of enemy. Of Japan, we may find it necessary to dispose once and for all, so that danger from that source may not again trouble the civilized world.

Japan has merited the most drastic treatment. Ever since she emerged from the darkness of the Middle Ages, about eighty years ago, Japan has been a danger to her neighbors.

By military threat and aggression, and by commercial chicanery, the Japanese have made themselves a general menace and a general nuisance. They have contributed nothing to the civilization into which they so suddenly intruded, save murder, fear and fraud. As a people, they have not a friend in the world. None who has been in any way associated with them is not the worse for that association.

The Germans have at least been for centuries a part of Europe, they have grown up alongside the rest of us, as a people if not as a political unit, and there seems some hope that they may be able to learn something from experience, so that they may at last assimilate themselves to the ways and the laws of an orderly world society. In the case of the Japanese, any such hope seems remote indeed.

Moreover, it may be said for the Germans that their industry and their skills are essential for a balanced European economy; Japanese industry is wholly unnecessary for a balanced Asiatic economy, which depends rather on the ability of the Chinese, the Indian and the other peoples of Asia to find their way toward the creation among themselves of the industry, the commerce and the political institutions suited to their needs. To this process of reconstruction and growth, the very presence of an interfering Japan is a menace which cannot be endured. The principle of the greatest good for the greatest number requires that this menace shall be removed, and that its removal shall be under such conditions that it shall have no opportunity of recurrence.

Fortunately, the facts of geography lend themselves to what may be called a semi-permanent solution of the problem thus presented. The islands of Japan, the home and center of the Japanese power, produce neither iron, nor copper nor oil, nor any save a very poor grade of coal. The Japanese difficulty may therefore be removed for good and all, at any rate for the lifetime of the next generation or so, by the complete and systematic destruction of Japanese industry.

This must be undertaken in no half-hearted manner. It must extend to the complete destruction of every industrial facility in all Japan, including railways and docks as well as manufacturing plants. It must extend to the removal from Japan of every machine tool, every mechanical device of every kind, every engine and motor, indeed every pound of metal, scrap or otherwise, which is capable of being made into such a thing, with the solitary exception of simple agricultural instruments, and possibly a few textile mills to be operated under the careful supervision of United Nations inspectors and guards.

Once this has been done, the people of Japan will find themselves incapable of injuring their neighbors. They will, indeed, find themselves under the necessity of tilling the soil of their islands with great industry and pursuing the vocation of fishermen, in order to survive at all.

There would be no mass starvation. The Japanese standard of living is not high, and while it would not improve, it could be maintained. There is still unused arable land in Japan proper, and the productivity of that which is now being tilled could be increased if the semi-feudal system of land tenure were altered in favor of more efficient methods. Rice forms 60% of the food of the Japanese people, and Japan imports only about 20% of her rice consumption; perhaps this deficit would have to be made up by the United Nations for a time, as part of the price we pay for security. Eventually the Japanese could build up the production for export of sufficient raw silk to buy their needs in rice, cotton and other basic necessaries. They would not be prosperous, but they would live after a fashion.

Of course, with the passage of time the excessive, indeed the artificially high population of Japan would tend to decrease. Already there are signs of a decrease in the Japanese birth-rate, as nature's solution for the problem of over-population. The Japanese will not emigrate. The best efforts of the Government over a period of ten years produced less than half a million total Japanese settlers in Manchukuo by the year 1941. The claim that foreign territory is needed to absorb the Japanese surplus of population is a mere myth, created out of whole cloth to cover up imperial ambitions. The Japanese population is high because the policy of Japan's leaders has been to encourage increase for military and industrial purposes. It will decrease when these pressures no longer exist, and return gradually to normal levels. This will probably occur before the doctrinaires of sweetness and light have brought about any change in our attitude toward the Japanese. We may at least hope so.

In their contacts with the outside world, the Japanese should be denied the use of their own ships. They will not be able to build metal ships, in any case, or airplanes; and if they build wooden vessels, these should be denied the right of entry at any United Nations port, with the possible exception of fishing vessels under due regulation. All contact with Japan should be by vessels of non-Japanese registry, entering designated ports under well regulated conditions, and discharging cargo into lighters. Any such vessel should be subject to libel, and the certificate of her master to revocation, if she carries to Japan any other article than the cargo stated in her manifest, which should be examined and certified by a United Nations officer at her last port of clearance before making for a Japanese port. It might be well to insist, at least for a time, on all such vessels carrying a United Nations inspector for the voyage from the last port of clearance to and from the Japanese port of destination. It might, indeed, be laid down that vessels proceeding to Japan must first enter and clear from certain designated ports—let us say, Shanghai, Vladivostok, Manila, Honolulu, Seattle and Weihaiwei.

It is difficult to see how, under these conditions, the Japanese could rebuild their industry, or come into possession of weapons or ships which would enable them to resume their criminal career. Thus simple and inexpensive police regulations would suffice to keep them in check, rather than the tremendously costly and burdensome armaments which every nation with possessions or interests in the Far East has been compelled to keep up for fear of Japanese aggression.

There is surely nothing offensive to the conscience of mankind in thus taking from the Japanese the modern weapons which they have not yet learned how to use save in the pattern of medieval brutality which rules their way of life. The restrictions suggested may be distasteful to seventy million Japanese, or what are left of them; but they are essential to the safety and progress of four hundred million Chinese, almost a like number of various Indian races, and a hundred odd million of the peoples of southeastern Asia and the adjacent islands: something like one-half the population of the world!

In so dealing with Japan, we shall moreover be assuring the security of East Asia and the Pacific by methods which may be carried into effect while popular sentiment in the various United Nations will still support them, and which cannot easily be undone by subsequent weakening of that sentiment.

It may be urged that it is unjust to treat the Japanese more drastically than the Germans, merely because the accidents of geography and the distribution of raw materials permit this to be done. But it must be recognized that in seeking the solution of these great problems, the process must be in part political, that is to say, taking into account the dictates of expediency, rather than wholly judicial. If Germany were an island, as devoid as Japan of natural resources, the world might benefit from inflicting on Germany the same fate as here proposed for Japan. This is not so. There are no available means, short of the ruthless extermination of the German people, of permanently keeping Germany in a state of subjection, though there are means of rendering Germany harmless for a time during which the reconstruction of world society along more cohesive and intelligent lines may be undertaken. That task will be immensely complicated if the restraint of Japan by similar methods must be undertaken at the same time. Those accidents of geography of which we have spoken fortunately permit the elimination of the Japanese danger during this period of strain and of reconstruction.

It is not necessary to argue that Japan's crimes are worse than Germany's, or vice versa. Both are equally guilty of outrages which might well be considered to merit extermination, so far as the dictates of justice are concerned. In neither country can the people who have supported and applauded these outrages, and served as the willing and indeed the enthusiastic instruments thereof, escape the moral responsibility for the crimes which their leaders have ordered, and which they have carried out or provided the means to carry out. The justice of the free nations, preserved by their own steadfast courage from the designs of these criminal states, may assuredly deal with these malefactors as the best good of humanity at large may require. In an enlightened society, criminal justice seeks rather the restoration and rehabilitation of the offender for whom there is any hope, than his destruction: save in those extreme cases when the death penalty may serve the purpose of example and of restraint on others. For Germany there may be some hope, given the existing conditions. For Japan there is far less, to judge from the record, and society is entirely justified in treating Japan with the extreme measures which in individual cases our laws reserve for the habitual criminal—measures which correspond to life imprisonment, with the possibility of pardon in the far distant future should circumstances seem to justify it. Moreover the fate of Japan may serve as an example and a warning to others who in the future may have the opportunity or the urge to live as Japan has lived, at the expense and by the conquest of their neighbors.

In particular, the fate of Japan may serve as an example to the German people, who will eventually come to realize that a similar degree of restraint upon themselves could only have been accomplished by their annihilation, and to understand that a repetition of their past crimes may bring exactly that penalty at the hands of an exasperated world community.

That this proposed destruction of Japanese power to injure others is not the perfect or the permanent solution of the whole problem, may be readily admitted. When all is said and done, it is a different scale of punishment than that which it is practicable to mete out to Germany, and it is different very largely because of differing conditions and not of differing deserts. But the jailing of one criminal, and the paroling of another, are neither of them perfect or permanent solutions of the relations of those men to society. The man who is jailed is not necessarily made better, he may be made worse. The man who is paroled does not necessarily become a reformed character because he has been leniently dealt with. He may commit a new crime before he has been out of the clutches of the law for an hour. Yet organized society has not yet devised a better means for dealing with its criminal elements than the application of its laws in this fashion. To put a criminal in jail does at least protect law-abiding citizens from his misconduct while he is behind bars. To release a promising offender on parole does at least give him a chance to show repentance and to become an asset to society instead of a liability, and some of them do so. These methods are the best that experience has taught us. They work in part, and in part they do not work. Human institutions cannot be expected to be perfect. We have at any rate come a long way from the time in which almost all criminals were ruthlessly put to death. We have likewise come a long way—as far as our own thinking is concerned, not that of the Germans or the Japanese—from the times when the people of a conquered state were massacred without pity, or carried off into slavery.

So we shall just have to deal with the Germans and with the Japanese on the best and most practicable plan that we can devise, for the greatest good of the greatest number of human beings, and in accordance not with ideals of abstract justice, but of what is possible and what promises best for the future within the limits of possibility.

We have now discussed our two major problems of disarmament as regards the enemy states which we are now fighting to subdue. It remains to examine what shall be done as regards their satellites, associates and accomplices.

Of these, the most important is Italy. There seems to be some prospect that the Italian people may earn some measure of rehabilitation by aiding the United Nations against Germany. The actual value of Italian aid has not been very great so far, as contrasted with the damage which Italian conduct has caused, especially to our Yugoslav and Greek allies, to say nothing of the long and evil heritage of Italian Fascism in the field of international relations. It seems likely that Italy should be kept under the same restraints as Germany with regard to the possession or manufacture of airplanes and ships of war. The economic restraints may be adapted to Italian conditions, and tempered in accordance with evidences of Italian good faith. Nothing could be more fatal than not to recognize such good faith if it really exists; on the other hand it might well be dangerous as well as unjust to take too much Italian good faith for granted.

With the Bulgarians it is hard to have any sympathy at all. They have twice backed the Germans when the Germans offered them the bait of aggrandizement at the expense of their neighbors, and conducted themselves with atrocious cruelty and arrogance when occupying their neighbors' territory. But it is hardly necessary to give any extended consideration to the problems of Bulgarian, Hungarian, Rumanian or Finnish disarmament, or of the disarmament of Thailand. None of these states is capable of manufacturing armaments of any consequence themselves. They are dangerous only as the dupes, the puppets or the accomplices of a greater power which is capable of putting weapons into their possession. If that is prevented, these small states can do little to threaten the peace of the world, and no great effort on the part of the United Nations will be required to keep them in reasonable order.

When the United Nations have accomplished the disarmament of Germany and Japan, and perhaps of Italy, they will have taken the first essential step toward the establishment of the peace of the world community. The known criminals will be under restraint. It will then remain for the law-abiding majority to find a means of preserving those restraints, of modifying them if need be, and of keeping its own members from falling out among themselves. There will remain, to be precise, the tremendous task of organizing and preserving the peace that victory has won. The disarmament of the criminal states can do no more than provide the opportunity to organize that peace without immediate fear of disturbance. It is an essential preliminary step, but it is only that. The major task will still lie ahead of us.

10. THE BEGINNINGS OF WORLD POLICE

We come now, to the end of the transition stage—the period of the disarmament of the enemy states, the period of temporary political authority by the United Nations Council in areas where local government is unable to function, the period of demobilization of the bulk of the United Nations fighting forces. How are we to pass from this stage to a settled condition of world-wide peace, maintained by the controlled and safeguarded use of force in the hands of the majority of human beings?

The real difficulty of creating such a system lies in finding a suitable means for the responsible application of force to maintain the common peace. It was the lack of such means that wrecked the League of Nations. That organization was dependent on the individual action of its member states to apply either military force or economic sanctions; it proved to have no real power to order timely remedial action. It could only make recommendations, which in general were not carried out. It has been generally assumed that the League should have had what is called an International Police Force, that is to say, a sort of independent, denationalized body of officers and men, equipped and armed from a common treasury, which could enforce the orders of international authority and act as the force behind the sanctions of international law.

But there are very great difficulties in the way of creating such a force. In the first place, it would be difficult to induce so great a number of men as would be required, to denationalize themselves, to abandon the loyalties of a lifetime, and to devote themselves wholeheartedly to the new cause of the impartial maintenance of peace. Then there would be the difficulty of supply; if the new force were to be able to fight when needed, and it would be worse than useless if it could not, then it would require as its support nothing less than the complete industrial support which any large fighting force needs in these days of total war. It might be possible to denationalize so many thousand men, and to arm and equip them so that they would make an imposing array; but you cannot denationalize the industry of all the member states of a world wide League, and without the support of industry no great fighting force can continue to fight very long.

The chief objection to an International Police Force on this model, however, seems to be the dangers inherent in its creation. Those who will seek to join it, and especially those who will seek to become officers in it, will be very largely men to whom a military career appeals of itself: not out of national loyalty, or national tradition, but men who love the soldier's trade, the pomp and circumstance of the profession of arms, the command of men, the prestige of rank. Such men, released from the restraints of the national loyalties they would have to forswear to enter the new force, might not find, in their newly assumed loyalty to a mere ideal, a sufficiently restraining influence upon their ambitions. Such men are the material of whom Napoleons and Wallensteins are all too easily made. Give into their hands the preponderance of armed power on this planet, and it might be found that the trusting nations had exchanged the peril of war for the certainty of slavery to a new and irresistible tyrant.

It is generally assumed by proponents of this form of international police force, that national disarmament by agreement on a grand scale will take place in parallel with the organization and establishment of the new police force. Unless this is so, the basic idea of the police force does not make sense, insofar as its use against any one of the member states of the association which supports it is concerned. If all the members maintain a considerable scale of armament, backed up by the national industrial strength, then the police force is just an extra fighting force, without industrial backing save such as may be allotted to it; and as against any member state, it becomes merely an addition to the national forces of the remaining states, though less efficient because it cannot have the same close administrative association with its sources of supply which national forces enjoy. Nothing is gained, in the military sense, that could not be had without the creation of the force as long as the major powers are agreed; if they fall out, the police force actually detracts from the ability of those who would restrain aggression to do so effectively, because it subtracts from the total amount of power which they can use at the highest level of efficiency. Moreover, the very existence of the international police force may cause the public at large, in some of the member nations, to entertain dangerous illusions of a security which does not in fact exist.

But, even making the very long assumption that all the major powers are now willing to disarm to the point where they would be helpless initially against attack by the international police force with its greater degree of immediate readiness for action, they would put themselves completely at its mercy in case it came under the wrong kind of leadership.

The truth seems to be, that as long as the major powers are in agreement, such an international police force might be useful, but as long as that is so the major powers can take care of the police of the defeated enemy states and of the general maintenance of order with their own forces. In that case, an internationalized force would only be an expensive and unsatisfactory instrument for the accomplishment of tasks which could be done better with the means normally at the disposal of the nations concerned.

To be entirely practical and realistic about all this, let us ask ourselves whether, after this war, we can imagine the people of the United States being willing to do away with the United States Navy, or to hand it over, in toto, to the control of an international agency? Obviously not. Nor can we imagine the British people so dealing with the Royal Air Force, which saved Britain in her hour of peril. Nor can we imagine the Russian people so dealing with the Red Army, of which they are so justifiably proud, and which is to so great an extent interwoven in the very warp and woof of the Russian national fabric.

It is unnatural that these things should be expected. They will not happen, and it is useless to imagine the establishment of international peace upon any such basis. Indeed, it is useless to think of international organization at all in the terms of some sudden, new, whole-cloth creation. It must be a natural growth, a development, proceeding from the sure foundation of known and trusted things, growing a little at a time and with each new growth subject to test and change. Only so may we build surely and safely for the future good of humanity.

That is true of the political organization, and it is likewise true of the police arm of that organization.

We have seen that, during the period of demobilization and disarmament, there will of necessity be in various parts of Europe and North Africa, in East Asia and the Pacific Islands, considerable elements of the naval, air and ground forces of various of the United Nations. For the most part, these forces will be operating under inter-allied commands, such as those of Eisenhower, MacArthur and Mountbatten. They will gradually be reduced in strength as demobilization proceeds, as the need for maintaining great establishments on the lines of communications lessens, as new governments arise which can maintain order in liberated or satellite territory, and as the disarmament of the enemy states becomes more definitely accomplished. As they are reduced in number, the character of these forces will change. It may be presumed that volunteers for a fixed period of foreign service will take the place of drafted men; temporary officers will be replaced by officers seeking a military career as a profession. The forces of occupation and police will assume more and more the character of professional, regular troops.

While this process is going on, the home governments of the powers to which these forces belong, will, as previously remarked, be engaged in determining the future character and strength of their peace establishments. They will have to take into account the need for maintaining the disarmament of the defeated enemy powers, including the continued occupation of enemy territory for such time as may be necessary; they will have to determine which of the innumerable naval and air bases scattered all over the world shall be demobilized and abandoned, and which shall be maintained in a state of immediate readiness, or in reserve, or devoted to purely commercial purposes; they will have to consider what dangers may arise in the future, against which their nations may require protection, and how those dangers may best be met, and with what scale of force. Most of these problems would be far more easily and simply solved if the basis for them be an international agreement in which the four principal powers of the United Nations take part. It seems certain that as a part, at least, of the national decisions on armament which must follow this war, there will be an agreement to maintain certain forces of occupation in former enemy territory for the time being, to maintain some of the far-flung air bases for the common use of all the agreeing powers (though perhaps dividing them up as far as actual occupation and administration is concerned), and that there must be some sort of agreement among the four powers concerned, and perhaps others, to act jointly in the case of the arising of certain defined and foreseeable emergencies.

From this it follows, altogether naturally, that the forces of occupation shall continue to be under international command, and that the commanders shall be immediately responsible to the Council of the United Nations, as representative of their governments. In other words, we shall find our United Nations police force, so far as occupation forces in enemy territory are concerned, ready made and functioning.

Its character will, however, be entirely different from the denationalized force which some students of this subject have imagined.

In the first place, it will not be composed of denationalized individuals. It will consist of Americans, Britons, Russians, Chinese and others, organized in units belonging to the armed services of those nations. The number of such units to be furnished by each nation will be determined by agreement, and it seems proper that such agreement should be subject to periodic re-examination in order to make adjustments due to changes in the situation. Certainly the American and British peoples, probably all the peoples concerned, will be reluctant to allow any great portion of their armed services to remain abroad except such as may volunteer for this duty. All of us are however accustomed to foreign service for officers and men of our regular establishments, and there seems little difference whether that foreign service be in the Philippines or in Germany. But it would seem advisable that the units serving under international control be periodically changed.

Next, as to command. Of course each troop unit and each air force unit will have its regular complement of officers, those properly belonging to it. They will not be commissioned in any international force, but will retain their commissioned status in the United States Army, or the British Army, or the Royal Air Force, or the Russian Army, and so on. They will simply be serving their country, as they are now, by helping to carry out certain obligations which their country has entered into for its own peace and security. As to general and staff officers, these should be detailed from the regular lists of such officers maintained on a permanent professional status by each nation concerned, and they should be detailed for restricted periods of time. In particular, no general officer or officer of comparable rank, and no general staff officer, should be allowed to serve with the international force for more than one year, or two years at the very outside limit.

This will prevent the growth of Napoleonic complexes, or their expansion into the field of action if they do develop. There is all the difference in the world between an officer who has no nationality, whose whole career and future is bound up with an international military organization under the direction of ever-changing political elements and forces, and—let us say—Major General X of the United States Army, whose career and future is under the control of his home government, whose loyalty is primarily to his own country and flag, and who is just on detail for a year or two years to a service where his country's needs require him to take under his temporary command some units belonging to other nations as well as his own, for the performance of carefully defined and established duties in a particular locality; whereafter he will return to his normal status as a general officer of his own army.

All of which, as previously pointed out, is a perfectly natural and reasonable development, and one which will take care of any difficulties or dangers which may arise from recalcitrance or unrest in occupied enemy territory. The forces maintained for this purpose need not be large, once enemy disarmament has been assured. They can be progressively reduced as the liberated states bordering on enemy territory grow stronger, and as the formation of new governments within enemy territory proceeds to the point where internal order can be maintained by such agencies.

Comparatively small elements of armored and motorized troops occupying well chosen central locations; infantry guards for air-fields and for dock areas in seaports; a proportion of air units sufficient for patrol and reconnaissance purposes, plus a small bomber and fighter reserve and a few squadrons of troop transports with parachutists and air infantry elements; and a fairly strong central reserve, perhaps of three or four divisions—this should be all that would be needed to control Germany for a time, once Germany has been properly disarmed. And even this force can be reduced in accord with improving conditions. If Japan is completely disarmed by the total destruction of her industry, as hereinbefore recommended, it may be possible to dispense with any force of occupation at all as soon as that destruction has been made complete; the troops of occupation may be able to march down to their ships alongside the last loads of outgoing metal scrap from the demolished factories and railways.

There will, however, be other calls for the services of United Nations armed forces. There will be problems in various colonial areas. What the political future of many of these areas will be, is as yet undetermined, and must be settled by political agreement. The mandated islands of the Pacific, Formosa, Korea and Italian Africa come under this head for discussion. While the discussion is going on, order must be maintained and some sort of provisional government established. This will be a United Nations responsibility, though it may be delegated to the power in actual occupation of the territory—for example, the British in Italian Africa, the United States or Australia in the Pacific islands. Thailand is a problem, too; so is Tangier; so are areas whose future status is in dispute, such as the Dodecanese Islands.

In former British colonies now under Japanese occupation, the British will be able to take over, at least until some general settlement of the colonial problem can be reached; it is not so certain that the Netherlands and France can do so at once. They may need help. The future status of Palestine will become a thorny problem as soon as the war ends. In none of these cases will large forces be needed; but in most of them, probably, the temporary presence of small United Nations forces will be absolutely essential. Remember, this is not a matter of keeping millions of young conscripts under arms; it is a matter of having a few regular soldiers on the spot when they are needed, lest a worse thing befall. It is not a matter of using American troops to force British, French or Dutch domination back upon the shoulders of millions of brown men, black men or yellow men; it is a matter of keeping order among those millions, of seeing to it that relief and rehabilitation services can operate, of getting transportation and communications systems into operation, of setting up public services of all sorts, and of upholding some sort of working government until the future status of all these areas can be settled by direct negotiation between the representatives of the peoples concerned and the occupying or administering powers, and between the governments of those powers themselves.

Finally, there comes the all-important matter of the police of the seas and of the airways. With the destruction of the German and the Japanese naval establishments, and the at least temporary eclipse of the Italian Navy, there remain only two really important world naval powers—the United States and the British Commonwealth of Nations. It may be expected that comparatively minor Russian and Swedish naval forces will continue to exist in the Baltic Sea, and Russian and Turkish naval forces in the Black Sea. Russia will likewise, doubtless, maintain some naval force based on her Pacific ports. But Russian naval power will be scattered, and of local rather than world consequence. Russia commands none of the various waters which connect her far-flung seaports, so she cannot concentrate her fleets in time of emergency. The French Navy will doubtless be rebuilt to some extent, and lesser powers will maintain small naval establishments for purposes of policing their home waters. There remain, however, the high seas, the vast ocean routes of the world over which so much of the world's commerce must continue to move. No enemy fleet will threaten this commerce in the immediate post-war period; and that no enemy shall arise to threaten it, must be the concern of the sea-power of the English-speaking nations.

Probably this can best be done by dividing the seas of the world into zones, for security purposes: the Pacific, the Western Atlantic and the Caribbean to the United States; the Eastern Atlantic, the Mediterranean and the Indian Ocean to the British, with special arrangements (perhaps a joint patrol with the Dutch) for the South China Sea. Of course, with the disappearance of the present dangers, there can be a considerable demobilization of British and American naval strength, and future naval building may well be conditioned by some international agreement which will prevent the rise of new threats to the security of the ocean highways, or provide against them if they do arise. This cannot be done by a single treaty, confining within rigid bounds the naval establishments of the contracting parties. It is rather a matter of continual review of the existing situation, and the adaptation to that situation of the means available to deal with it. This is just another example of the need for political unity among the great powers, and of the fact that such political unity must exist if any combined military arrangements are to be practicable.

It is worthy of note, that an adequate system of bases for the naval control of the world's oceans is already in the possession of the English-speaking powers. Besides bases on the home territory—the Continental United States and the British Isles—there are Gibraltar, Malta, Cyprus and Aden, as to the Mediterranean; Colombo, Cape Town, Fremantle and Mauritius, as to the Indian Ocean; Pearl Harbor, Dutch Harbor, Samoa, and one or two of the mandated islands, as to the Pacific; Singapore and a base to be arranged for in the Philippines, as to the South China Sea; and Panama, Trinidad and Puerto Rico as to the Caribbean. The North Atlantic is dominated by Britain, Canada and the eastern seaboard bases of the United States, though a base in Iceland may be essential; the South Atlantic is controlled by Cape Town, Freetown, and the Falklands to some extent though it would be better if we had a standing arrangement with Brazil about the use of some port near her outward shoulder, and with the French as to the use of Dakar.

It should of course be no part of United Nations policy, or of American or British policy, to prevent smaller powers from having a measure of naval strength. Limitations on naval strength in the case of small nations usually arise from natural causes, such as budgetary and ship-building capacities. Wherever it appears that any state is building for aggressive purposes, that may be a proper subject for appropriate action by the United Nations Council, and of that action the American and British fleets may become the instrument; but they would then be acting as the agents of the majority of mankind, for the preservation of the common peace, and not to oppress or abuse a helpless little state. In discussions of naval limitations among larger states, it will doubtless be found wise to examine periodically the naval establishments and appropriations of all the larger United Nations, but there seems no reason why such adjustments as may be mutually agreed upon cannot be made without undue friction.

As to the police of the airways, this must become a matter of international regulation—again on a flexible and continuous basis, not on the basis of rigid treaty agreement. The close of this war will mark the beginning of a tremendous increase in commercial aviation, on a world wide basis. The possibilities are unbounded: they go far beyond the confines of even our present soaring imaginations. The security of air transport is just as important to the future peace and well-being of the world, as the security of maritime transport: if not more so. Its regulation must be the subject of careful study and constant attention. On routes which traverse the oceans, the security of the air lanes may well be made, for the time being at any rate, the responsibility of the great sea powers. In other areas, as may be appropriate, that responsibility will be shared with Russia, China, and perhaps France and the Netherlands, as to European and Asiatic lines; and with Latin American powers over their own territories.

There should be no confusion of thought as between this question of the security of international air lanes, and the proper exercise of domestic police power by sovereign states, large or small, over airplanes landing in the national territory or passing over it. It is the established right of any country today, to make regulations governing the entrance and clearance from its ports of foreign merchant vessels, and foreign men-of-war as well, to require compliance with police, health and customs regulations, to exact the payment of various fees, and to require the compliance of officers and men of such ships with local laws. It would, however, be considered a grossly unfriendly act for any state arbitrarily to bar from its ports vessels flying the flag of another state. It is furthermore well recognized that on the high seas, the ships of all countries are subject not only to the laws of their own land, but to established international law as far as it apples to particular cases. A similar reasoning may well be applied to international air traffic. In practise, in the post war world, the United States and Great Britain will be almost alone in possessing the power to police the high seas; and in practise, in the post-war world, the great powers within their several spheres of interest and strength, will alone possess the ability to police the air lanes. That should never be allowed to mean that the smallest sovereign state cannot make proper regulations for the local control of air traffic. However, just as international maritime traffic is controlled by a set of regulations to which, in general, the maritime nations have all agreed, so international air traffic will have to be regulated by an International Air Authority on which every state will have due representation; and it will not be proper for these regulations, when agreed upon, to be set at defiance by municipal law or regulation, which must confine itself to procedures properly within the framework of the international agreements.

Finally, it must be recognized that long-range bombing aircraft, and long-range planes capable of carrying air infantry or parachutists, are instruments of force capable of spanning enormous distances in a very short time, and of being quickly concentrated at any point in the world where the use of force may be needed, no matter what their areas of origin. This process will of course be immensely facilitated if there exists a world-girdling system of air bases at the disposal of the forces thus desiring to concentrate airborne striking power. As to a great part of the world, such a system of bases already exists and is in the possession of the United States and the British Commonwealth. These are also the nations which have gone farthest in developing the long-range aircraft as an instrument of war. They will have a great advantage over other states in this respect for some time to come after war is over, because of their possession not only of experience in the operation and maintenance of such aircraft, but of production facilities. This is a fact which must be taken into account in any system of world police. Naval power plus long-range air power can form, so to speak, an excellent fire department which can be rushed to any spot where the first sign of conflagration may be detected. Again, this does not call for the maintenance of enormous military establishments; it does call for the maintenance of adequate and immediately ready establishments, kept fully up to date by constant change and addition, and manned by thoroughly trained personnel; and it requires the maintenance of a system of bases capable of giving full mobility to the air and naval forces of the powers concerned, and adequately guarded against such scale of attack as conditions may make possible.

In all these matters, it will be noted that no great new international structure, whether military or political, is required. What is really essential is the over-riding political agreement, to make common use for common ends of the forces which will already exist. It would be a real calamity if this opportunity were missed, and if, in consequence, these questions of military power had to be settled by each government in accordance with its own view of its own needs, and without examining the possibilities of cooperation with its neighbors and associates.

We have, however, been concerned in this chapter only with what may be called the beginnings of world police. We have tried to show the first steps in developing a system of world police from the conditions and forces that will exist as the demobilization period draws to a close, and as problems of domestic as well as international political and economic adjustments become paramount in men's minds, instead of the dreadful problems of war. We have yet to examine how this developing system, this natural outgrowth of the conditions of victory, can be made permanent, or at least can be given life, and can become operative under conditions which will assure us of security from war and the fear of war for a generation or two.

11. THE FOUNDATIONS OF PEACE

THE REAL FOUNDATIONS of peace, the peace of the world community, must consist, not in weapons, in armed forces, in the instruments of power, nor yet in treaties and pacts and Senate resolutions, but in the hearts and souls of men and women everywhere on this planet, in the profound conviction that peace is necessary, in the profound faith that it is attainable, and in the unshakable determination to possess and to preserve it.

The end of the war will bring upon the peoples of the United Nations a period of terrific reaction. Everyone, everywhere, will want to forget the horrors through which we have passed. Everyone, everywhere, will want to get back as quickly as possible to "normal" ways of life. Everyone, everywhere will have a false sense of having escaped a great danger which cannot conceivably return, of having come safely through the raging storm into haven. Such a period of reaction wrecked the peace that might have been constructed in the years that followed World War I. It is the lesson which that failure and its result have taught us, that gives us our best hope that this time the reaction, though it will come, will not have the same effect.

But it is important, it is perhaps vitally important, that we should have at hand and visibly in operation, those agencies of world police and political unity among the nations, of which the preceding chapters have treated. They are the signs which all can see, which are not only necessary in themselves but are symbols of hope for the future. They are, however, in a sense, the continuation of war and of war conditions. They may have within them the seeds of permanence, but those seeds must be permitted to flower into the actuality and also the appearance of permanence. In other words, we must make war instruments into peace instruments; a war system, being victorious, must become a peace system to preserve that victory, and it must be so recognized by all who behold it.

The difficulty lies in this, that peace is not to be had without force; that the application of force, in international affairs, is for great powers only, small powers being without the means to create and maintain the instruments of force; and that, therefore, our war system, projected past the hour of victory into the future, begins to have the appearance of a military dictatorship over the lesser powers by the greater, because armaments (even though modest in actual peacetime establishment) are, in the hands of a great industrial power, so immensely more formidable in potential threat than any means of defense which a small power can ever hope to possess.

The disparity between the means of defense of the small power, and the means of offense of the great power, is in some sense like the disparity between the peaceful citizen and the power of government in any established community. The government has an army, a navy, an air force; it has police of various sorts; against it the citizen is defenseless, if it be considered merely as an irresponsible tyranny over which he has no control. Yet the possession of armed forces by governments is necessary for the maintenance of domestic peace, and for the security of the state against aggression. Therefore men who would be free, and yet secure against common enemies both foreign and domestic, have contrived means by which governments may be armed, and yet the unarmed citizen may be safe in life, liberty and the pursuit of happiness. This is what is meant by the supremacy of the civil over the military power, which is the foundation of constitutional government in the United States and throughout the British Commonwealth.

We are very far, indeed, from any sort of world government which can realize Tennyson's dream of the Parliament of Man, the federation of the world.

But we must realize that we are now making the revolution which will in God's good time bring such a world government into being.

We are all too accustomed to think of Fascism and Nazism as being—as their leaders claim—the "new order," something which has suddenly sprung up out of primeval slime to horrify and torment the world.

Nothing could be farther from the truth. Nazism and Fascism are but the last and dreadful struggle of the ancient forces of authoritarian rule, of the concept which once was called the divine right of kings, of the theory that the many must be governed by the wisdom and for the benefit of the few. The revolution against this idea has been growing stronger as man has grown in knowledge; our own Revolution was a part of it; today we find the free peoples of the world banded together in one of the final acts of the greater revolution which will end in freedom and peace for all mankind—freedom under law, peace under the sword of justice.

The makers of a revolution of such origins and such purposes must act responsibly when the power is in their hands, when the forces of tyranny lie prostrate. They must act, not as Napoleons, seizing the trappings of empire from the bayonets of an adoring soldiery, but as Washingtons, brushing aside proffered crowns and asking only to be allowed to serve the public good. This is the responsibility which will lie upon the great powers of the United Nations—the United States, the British Commonwealth, Russia and China—when this war is over.

How is this responsibility to be met?

Let us see, first, what the conditions may be, as the need for translating temporary war-time agencies into permanent peace-time institutions grows more pressing.

We shall probably have certain United Nations armed forces in Germany, others in various parts of what is now occupied or satellite Europe. These will be under inter-allied command. They will be much reduced from their former numbers, and they will be composed in great part of volunteer troops, except perhaps the Russian contingents. We shall likewise have certain United Nations forces in various parts of East Asia, under similar conditions. The seas of most of the world will be patrolled by American and British men-of-war, possibly under an arrangement dividing the duties of patrol between the two nations as already discussed. All these military forces will be controlled through the Combined Chiefs of Staff at Washington, or through agreement between the Combined Chiefs of Staff and the Russian High Command, if the Russians have not come into the C.C.S. On their home territory, all the United Nations will have various armed forces in the process of demobilization, and the beginnings of the new, permanent, armed forces forming their newly recreated peace establishments, of which most of the units serving beyond their borders will have become parts.

The Germans, the Japanese and their satellites will be totally disarmed. Neutral states will retain some degree of armament, as their needs and their pocketbooks may permit; but the disappearance of the Axis peril will probably cause the demobilization of a great part of the neutral armed strength.

There will also exist a number of international, or at least United Nations agencies of various sorts. There will have to be some sort of European Transportation Authority, and a Communications Authority also. There will be the United Nations Relief and Rehabilitation Administration, which will be working all over the world. There will be a Food Authority, and a Shipping Authority, and a Commercial Aviation Authority. All of these will have to work closely together, and their work will have to be coordinated, so that we must assume that sheer necessity will have brought into being an over-riding political agency, a United Nations Council such as we have previously discussed. Of this Council, the existing Pacific War Council and Mediterranean Council, and the advisory Council on European Affairs to be created under the provisions of the Moscow pacts, seem likely to be the germs and perhaps the original components, or supporting sub-agencies.

It is not to be supposed that the Council can be given direction of military operations while the war is going on, but when it is over, when our enemies have surrendered, it seems quite essential that the Council should gradually come to be considered as the political supervisor, so to speak, of the Combined Chiefs of Staff. We will then have, at least in embryo, the proper relationship of the civil to the military power.

We have already discussed the composition of the Council, and the relationships within it of great powers to small powers. How this will work out in practise, only time will show. But it is important that we do as much as we can while the war is still in progress, that we move step by step toward the objective of the war not only by military victories, but by political accomplishments also.

It is not to be expected that the Council will be the only agency by which relations between the sovereign states composing it may be carried on. The normal processes and functions of diplomacy will continue. States will make agreements one with another, such as the Soviet-British alliance, and the new Soviet-Czechoslovak alliance. As long as the purposes of these arrangements are consistent with the common purposes of the United Nations, such arrangements will strengthen rather than weaken the greater structure. It should be part of the work of the United Nations Council to prevent contradictions from arising, and to weave into a common pattern all these threads uniting the various states.

All of which, it may be said by doubting Thomas, are fine words representing noble aspirations. But just how much authority is to be given to this Council, and just how is it to carry out its task of maintaining world peace without violating the principle of national sovereignty?

In other words, precisely what is this thing which is being proposed?

Frankly, friend Thomas, it is a stop-gap, an improvisation, a compromise with the ideal. It is in cold and sober truth a *modus vivendi*, very literally a means of living—a means by which our civilization may get through the difficult period from the end of this war until the opportunities of peace have enabled men's minds to devise something better, and distilled enough of hatred and fear out of men's blood so that they will accept something better and make that something work.

In detail, its purposes may be stated as follows:

(1) To prevent the Germans and the Japanese, known to be nations of criminal record and intent, from rearming themselves and again disturbing the peace of the world.

(2) To prevent, as far as possible, the arising of any other threat to that peace from any other quarter.

(3) To accustom the United Nations to working together for the accomplishment of common ends, and to provide a means by which they can conveniently do so.

How are these purposes to be accomplished?

We must begin by the assumption that the United States, the nations of the British Commonwealth, Russia and China will constitute themselves as what might be called the senior wardens of the new peace, and that they will by agreement among themselves maintain certain elements of their armed forces ready at all times for use in dealing with threats to peace. As already remarked, these forces need not be large ones, as long as no considerable threat is permitted to accumulate.

Let us first consider the measures necessary for the restraint of Germany. The British will probably maintain in the United Kingdom certain air and naval units; the Russians will keep a certain number of divisions in permanent garrisons along their western frontier, certain air units at western stations, and, no doubt, a fleet of modest size in the Baltic. One more step seems wise and necessary, at the point where the occupation forces in the key centers in Germany are to be withdrawn.

It seems advisable that there should be immediately and permanently at hand a small but thoroughly alert preventive force under the immediate direction and at the instant call of the United Nations Council, to deal with any violation of the disarmament restrictions which may be imposed on Germany. The ideal location for such a force is in the Schleswig-Holstein peninsula, where it could guard a neutralized Baltic Canal which should be freely open to the commerce of all nations, where it could keep watch over Germany's principal contacts with the overseas world through the ports of Hamburg and Bremen, and where it could be within immediate striking distance of Berlin. It is therefore suggested that the territory between the Danish frontier and a line south of, parallel to and fifteen miles distant from the Baltic canal be placed under United Nations administration, with local self-government under a civil administrator (neither a German nor a Dane) appointed by the United Nations Council, and that in this territory be located a system of air bases, occupied by a mixed force of American, Russian and British air force units to include heavy bombardment, fighter and observation sqaudrons and air transport elements, and that this territory be garrisoned by a ground force of three or four divisions—one American, one British, one Russian, and possibly one air-borne division furnished by all three states. These should be organized as a complete army corps, and should include a strong proportion of armored and motorized units. The commander should be changed every year or two years, and the command should rotate among the supporting powers, as should the principal staff appointments. A naval patrol force based on Kiel should cooperate with this garrison.

It is submitted that such a force would be ample to keep a disarmed Germany in check insofar as small embryonic violations of the conditions of German disarmament might be concerned—provided it were instantly and ruthlessly used at the first sign of trouble. It seems likely that only one or two examples would have to be furnished recalcitrant Germans of readiness to use this force, whereafter its mere existence would be a sufficient deterrent. It could be quickly supported, if necessary, from Russia and the British Isles.

Under what authority would it act? It would seem necessary that discretion as to its use be vested in the United Nations Council, so that reference back to the constituent governments would not be necessary. Indeed, it would be better if the great powers concerned would earmark certain of their home units (the British air and naval units, and the units permanently stationed in West Russia, above mentioned, and perhaps certain American units in Eastern bases) to be likewise at the disposal of the Council by a permanent arrangement, or better, by an annually renewed arrangement with full legal and constitutional sanction behind it. The Germans must not be allowed again to put their trust in the slowness with which their intended victims react to the first steps in aggression, or the unreadiness of those victims to use forcible means to protect themselves.

Of course the other neighbors of Germany will keep up armaments to some extent. Poland is especially important in this connection, because Poland lies between Russia and Germany. There must be no question as to Polish willingness to take part in the police of Germany, or to permit the passage of Russian troops and planes when the United Nations Council may so order: Poland being, of course, a member state of the Council. The same considerations, varying in importance with geographical position, apply to Holland, Belgium, France, Denmark and Czechoslovakia.

It seems altogether probable that the actual need for what may be called international police in Europe can be satisfied: (1) By the maintenance of the comparatively small force above described in Schleswig-Holstein; (2) The "ready" contingents of Russian and British forces, and perhaps some smaller contributions from other powers, all at the call of the United Nations council when need be; (3) The support of these forces, and the assurance of their communications, by the air and sea power of Great Britain and the United States on the Atlantic side and in the Mediterranean, and the air and sea power of Russia within the Baltic.

Under such conditions of security, the tendency would be for most European states to maintain only minimum armaments, and to devote the greater part of their resources to building up their commerce, their industry, their social and educational services, and in general to promoting the public welfare. It would be the task of the various international agencies in these fields to promote better relations and closer cooperation, and to prevent the setting up of customs and police barriers, as far as possible, which would interfere with the free flow of trade and the free movement of individuals.

Here, at least, we have a beginning for our brave new Europe, and our brave new world.

As to the guard over Japan: in the naval sense, that will be the responsibility of the United States, save as to Russian naval detachments inside the Sea of Japan. The island base system Hawaii-Midway-Guam, with Dutch Harbor as northern outpost, and with a base in the Philippines by arrangement, will suffice for the purposes of naval control over Pacific waters. The Sea of Japan can be left to the Russians. But the Yellow Sea and the Strait of Tsushima remain, and also the need for an air base close to Japan's home territory—just "in case". This might best be obtained by arrangement with whatever government may be established in Korea, so that somewhere close to the end of the Korean peninsula a few patrolling squadrons might be established to maintain watch and ward over Japan. Probably southern Sakhalin will go back to Russia, and a shuttle base might be established there. There would be little need for a large garrison of ground troops—a mixed division would be enough, a force merely adequate to deal with, say, a "forlorn hope" assault by desperate Japanese in a swarm of fishing boats. The garrison should be American, British and Chinese, with the Russians garrisoning the shuttle station in Sakhalin.

There is your world police system—with the essential addition of the world-girdling system of British and American air and naval bases, plus the maintenance by Russia and China of land forces adequate to guarantee the peace of the vast Eurasian land mass which they inhabit, and lesser forces by lesser powers adequate to maintain their own domestic peace and their safety from purely local aggressions by neighbors of like estate.

It isn't very formidable, this system. It isn't very expensive. It won't mean the stationing of millions of American youth abroad—just a division plus in Schleswig-Holstein, a regiment or two in Korea, a few scattered air squadrons, a few naval base garrisons (mostly Marines) and air-base guard detachments, and the Navy. It will mean the obligation to keep these forces up to strength, fully armed, trained and equipped, ready to act at the drop of a hat; and it will mean keeping up a certain armed strength in the United States and its outlying territories, as a reserve. But it certainly will not take more of our revenue than we can comfortably allot to purposes of national defense, and it will provide a far better insurance against war than any unilateral wall-building system we can devise or support, besides being far less expensive in both man-power and dollars.

It will work, and it will make us secure. But it will work only as long as it is properly used, properly controlled, surrounded with adequate safeguards and supported by the general confidence of all concerned.

At this point, doubting Thomas will have another question. It is all very well to disarm the Germans and the Japanese, and then sit on them with a few planes and soldiers; but how about the rest of the world? How are you going to prevent war breaking out between some of the other powers?

That requires us to take a broad general look, first of all, at the military balance of the world under the proposed arrangement.

We will have two great naval and air powers, in close contact with each other at many points throughout the world, jointly policing the seas and much of the world's air. These powers are the United States and the British Commonwealth of Nations. Traditionally, these countries do not maintain large armies, and there will, under the conditions stated, be little need for them to do so in the post-war period.

We will also have two great land powers, in close contact with each other along the world's longest land frontier—Russia and China. Russia will be in a far more advanced state of political, military and industrial development than China, but both will have enormous internal problems to be dealt with.

This produces a sort of equilibrium of power. The Anglo-American sea and air power, with its insular bases, will be unable to get at, or inflict serious injuries upon the Russian land power, or the Chinese land power either, when that nation becomes better organized. It is in fact doubtful, as Clausewitz pointed out long ago, whether a great continental empire can ever be conquered. Both Napoleon and Hitler tried, and failed, to conquer Russia; and Japan has been unable to subdue China after seven years of intensive struggle and every possible technical advantage.

On the other hand, neither the Russian nor the Chinese land power can get at, or inflict serious injury upon the sea and air power empires of Britain and America. The Germans, much better placed than the Russians for so doing, could not conquer Britain when Britain stood alone, though they added air superiority to an overwhelming land superiority. Napoleon's imperial progress was always checked and turned back by the power of the sea. Today, it is only in combination with the land power of Russia that America and Britain are beating Germany; and in 1918, they were able to do so only in combination with the land power of France and Italy.

Therefore the natural course to take, is for the continental powers to cooperate with the insular powers; for (to reduce the problem to its lowest level of self-interest) neither can conquer the other, and therefore they must find a way of getting along. "If you can't lick 'em, jine 'em."

There remains the danger that the two sea and air powers may fight each other, or the two continental powers. But if we are to envisage a world in which an Anglo-American war can even be conceivable, it is a world so far gone in folly, in departure from all principle and all possibility of cooperation, that it is a world already foredoomed. Perish the thought, even in imagination. Indeed, there is every reason to hope than an increasing degree of Anglo-American solidarity, including political and economic as well as military association of the closest kind, may be one of the strongest pillars of the new world structure.

The one real danger, and it is a danger which cannot be

shrugged aside, is the chance of war between Russia and China. Against that danger, the safeguards are these:

(1) The very Anglo-American solidarity of which we have just spoken, expressing itself in common action—by diplomacy, through the various United Nations agencies, and on the economic front—to bring about and to preserve good relations between our two great continental allies.

(2) The extremely difficult transportation conditions along most of the Russo-Chinese frontier, so that even should hostilities break out, they would progress slowly at first, and there would be opportunities for the good offices of other powers to take effect before irreparable damage were done.

(3) The very grave internal problems which Russia and China must each solve, and which will, or should, absorb most of the energies and wisdom of both peoples for some years to come.

But, doubting Thomas may argue, what is to prevent Russia from building up an enormous sea and air power, to supplement her land power—and then setting out to conquer both Europe and Asia, and eventually the world, from her strong interior position?

Well, that is the bogey with which Dr. Goebbels has been trying to terrify the world for some years past. The Bolshevik menace. Russia, freed of restraint by the defeat of Germany and Japan, setting out to subdue us all.

In fact, Russia cannot easily become a great sea power. Her sea frontiers are widely separated—the Baltic Sea, the Arctic, the Sea of Japan, the Black Sea. In the past Russian naval policy has been to maintain a small naval force in each of these locations. Russian naval power in sum total has been respectable, but it has never been strong enough to do very much at any one point. But the real difficulty, the real fallacy in the "Red menace" argument lies deeper. No power in history has ever, since the decline of the Roman Empire, been able to be a great sea power and a great land power at one and the same time. Spain tried it, but though Spain became formidable on land, at sea she was always contemptible when faced by real seamen such as the British or the Dutch. France under Louis XIV lost an empire because her efforts were always divided between naval-colonial progress and continental wars. The France of Napoleon could never create a real sea-power. The Germany of William II tried to be formidable by sea and by land, and only succeeded in drawing upon herself the enmity of the world, while her great fleet rusted away in harbor—though the effort expended on it might, applied to the army, have made the difference between continental victory and defeat. Japan today is exhausting herself in the last stages of a vain struggle, because, being a maritime empire, she has nevertheless seen fit to engage in a program of continental conquest. Britain did the same thing during the Hundred Years' War, and never rose to world power and influence until the stupid attempt to conquer France was finally abandoned.

The truth of the matter seems to be that the proportion of the national resources which can be devoted to armament is limited, as to any given nation or people however naturally wealthy, and that this proportion cannot be exceeded without weakening the fabric and foundation of the state to such an extent that the over-grown armaments cannot be supported and kept in operation for any lengthy period of time. Thus—on the basis of historical experience—one can say with confidence that Russia cannot maintain great land armies as she does today, supported by a strong tactical air force, and still afford to add to these a great strategical long-range air force, and a great sea power. And one can further say that should Russia—even great, rich Russia—seek to create such a triple-barreled instrument of conquest, it would break down of its own weight. It could not keep going against the accumulating resistance of the rest of the world, because the resources even of Russia would not be sufficient to support it: and because the very fact and strain of its creation and preparation would have already undermined the foundations of healthy, vigorous nationhood. Russian soldiers fight magnificently today because they are fighting in a holy cause. They fight best, as they have always fought best, in defense of the soil of their fatherland. The slogans which inspire them are the slogans of a free people hurling an invader from their hearths and homes. All this cannot be changed in a twinkling into a lust for conquest and for the enslavement of others.

The military basis of the new peace is assured, because there exists an equilibrium of distributed power among the principal states, and because the interests of those states are far more engaged in maintaining peace than in disturbing it. The conditions may usefully be compared, though they are not the same, with those of the Pax Britannica, when Britain could not directly attack any of the states of continental Europe because she had no army, and no continental state could attack Britain because none of them had real naval power. Under those conditions, Britain was able to keep the peace which her self-interest demanded, because her sea power could hurt the interests of her neighbors and probably in the end be decisive in a war between them; and Britain took care always to maintain at least a good understanding with one or more strong continental powers—Prussia and Austria at one time, Germany at another, then France and finally France and Russia. In like manner the new alliance, or rather the new senior warden's association to guarantee the future of the United Nations, will marry sea and air power to land power, and keep a balance between the two.

Here, then, are the military foundations of peace, and we have already described the distribution of force which will enable any threat to peace to be dealt with.

It is, however, apparent that there must be unity at the top—unity of policy and purpose among all the United Nations, in order that peace may continue, may be fruitful, and may at long last develop into something resembling Tennyson's dream —the true Parliament of Man.

The original instrument of this political unity will be the United Nations Council. It will probably be, in great part, an advisory council and a discussion group: at least at first. It will have acquired much experience, we may hope, in the adjustment of difficult international problems during the war and the demobilization period. But its powers will not in all matters be clearly defined, and they may not have any accurate relation to the constitutional structures of the member states.

This last condition calls for definite correction. Each member state should, by appropriate action in accordance with its own fundamental law, empower its executive to take part in the deliberations of the Council, and to use the armed forces of the nation in participating, with other states, in carrying out the decisions of the council relating to the disarmament of the late enemy states and in dealing with such other threats to the peace of the world as may engage the attention of the Council.

To be more specific, this arrangement as applied to the United States might involve an amendment to the Constitution, reading somewhat as follows:

> "The President is empowered, under such basic conditions as the Congress may approve, to enter into a permanent arrangement with other nations for the specific purpose of maintaining the peace of the world; and to designate such elements of the regular armed forces of the United States as he may select, to be subject to the call of such international organization as the United States may join, for the suppression of threats to that peace, subject to the prior approval of the President in each case where the active employment of such forces may be required.
>
> "It is specifically recognized, that such action by the

United States, and by the armed forces thereof, as may be carried out under the terms of this Article, is a proper exercise of the responsibility of the American people for taking their due share in keeping the general peace of the world, and does not constitute an act or acts of war.

"The President shall annually, upon the convening of the Congress next after the first day of each calendar year, make a full report to the Congress of all actions taken by him under the provisions of this Article, and of the number and location of the armed forces of the United States serving outside the territory thereof."

This amendment attempts to give constitutional recognition to the principle upon which the whole peace structure of the future must rest, if it is to be effective: that what action may be taken by the duly authorized representatives of the majority of mankind to keep the common peace does not constitute "going to war" with the nation or people which are the source of danger, but is, in principle, police action, by continuously maintained, legally recognized agencies which have a right to command the loyal cooperation of all law-abiding peoples and individuals.

Therefore, under the proposed amendment, it would not be necessary for the President to ask Congress for a declaration of war against Germany, for example, in order to use the armed forces of the United States to smash an illegal German airplane factory. He could do a great many things which he cannot legally do now, provided he did them in cooperation with other powers, and under the general authority of the United Nations Council. The Council could not, however, order the armed forces of the United States into action without the approval of the President. That approval might be given in advance, to cover specific conditions which could be foreseen; but the fears expressed by some opponents of international organization, that "the United States would have to go to war at the behest of foreigners" would have no foundation in fact under such a system.

The whole purpose of the system would indeed be to prevent the United States from ever having to go to war at all, by using a minimum of force in a timely and regular manner to destroy the germs of war wherever they might be perceived, and before they might multiply to dangerous proportions.

Presuming that the other powers concerned would take appropriate action similar in purpose to the Constitutional amendment suggested above for the United States, there would always be at the disposal of the Council sufficient force to act effectively and promptly in the face of nascent peril.

These forces would not be of the character of the "international police force" of which so many post-war planners have dreamed. They would not be unreservedly at the disposal of an international authority for use against any state which might be considered by others an "aggressor." There is little likelihood that any such state of affairs could be reached in the immediate future, or ought to be reached. What does seem well within the bounds of possibility is the use of forces of specified size, for specific purposes under treaty agreements, and the assignment to these forces of units of the regular military establishments of the contributing nations for periods of time and under conditions of command and administration previously agreed upon. This is well within the limits of our present war experience, and can usefully be continued into the post-war period, as long as there is never any doubt in anyone's mind as to exactly what is being done, and why, and for whose benefit.

Behind these special forces, behind the whole police system, would stand the united strength of the great powers, and the full support of the lesser powers who will be members of the United Nations, just as the full strength and resources of the whole community stand behind the lone patrolman facing, in the dead of night, a robber lurking in a dark alleyway. This is the essence of police action, as contrasted to war action. Police action is most effective when it is preventive, when it does not have to shoot; war action is merely the final sacrifice which has to be made because there has been no effective means of preventing the evil from getting out of hand. The enlightened community does not let criminals run wild until they can only be dealt with by calling out the militia, and declaring a state of martial law.

It is not pretended that the suggested system of world police is perfect, or that it will prevent all wars forever after. In some cases it may not be able to prevent wars between lesser states from breaking out. But it can certainly go into action to confine those wars to their original locales, to keep other states from joining in, to exercise upon the conduct of those wars the ameliorating pressure of a great body of world opinion, and to bring them to an end as quickly as possible. It is by no means proposed that, should Rumania and Hungary for example fly at each other's throats, American troops should be dispatched to the Balkans to make them stop fighting. It is, however, proposed that the Council should immediately recommend to its member states such parallel diplomatic and economic action as would prevent any of the neighboring states from taking sides, and would prevent either of the belligerents from getting any supplies or assistance from outside sources until they did stop fighting.

Under such conditions, one may venture to think that small wars would not last very long.

If there is no possible guaranty against the outbreak of small international wars, there is certainly none against the incidence of civil war. This too has been a danger to the peace of the world in times past; the unhappy example of Spain is all too fresh in our memories. If the people of any land can find no other way of reconciling their differences than bloody recourse to internal strife, their neighbors may deplore the fact, they may use all their influence to prevent it, but they can hardly be justified in intervening by force. What organized society outside the troubled state can do is to prevent the taking of sides by other nations, as in Spain, or the seizing of the opportunity by the rapacious to deprive the war-torn state of its possessions. Civil war is a matter domestic to the state in which it takes place; the intervention of any other state by force of arms, or even the unilateral application of economic sanctions, must bring with it greater perils to the peace of the world community than the fiercest internal struggle within a single state. However, it must be recognized that this, like all hypothetical questions, cannot be viewed entirely in the abstract; that the good of the majority must rule; and that there may well be instances in which the United Nations, acting as a community and not singly, might be justified in taking drastic steps to prevent the spread of a civil war outside the confines of the state in which it originated, and especially to prevent it assuming in any degree an international character.

At all times and in all circumstances, the international sale of weapons, munitions and material of war should be under closest scrutiny of the Council. It might well be provided that an agency of the Council should examine all such sales or transfers, and that they should not be permitted to take place until the Council has approved them. It would not do to forbid them altogether, since many small states would thereby be deprived of essential weapons for the maintenance of their domestic peace.

All of this is, of course, only a beginning. It is, as already remarked, a makeshift—a means of keeping peace in the world until men can devise a better one. It is not a world government, for such a government must deal through constitutional machinery with individuals; it cannot deal with sovereign states unless they cease in part to be sovereign. It is just a device in order to gain that breathing space without which none of our dreams for the future can ever come true.

This is the great need of the present: that the world shall have, after its terrible travail of the past quarter-century, an interval of security from war, an interval in which men may lift up their heads and hearts to contemplate their future, and to find a way to make that future one of promise and not of terror. If the suggestions of this book have any virtue, it is that they seek the accomplishment of this end by the development of known and trusted ways and things and institutions, and not by the sudden creation of a new and wondrous edifice in which none can have confidence because it is unlike anything which men have known about before.

Of course we must keep our ideals before us. Of course we must look forward to a future of better things, and closer bonds between man and man as between nation and nation. Of course we must try to see on the far horizon the dawn of that true brotherhood of man which shall forever mark the end of war, and which perhaps our great grandchildren, if they are given the chance, may come actually to realize. But we must not imperil that chance by trying now to do more than lies within our means to accomplish.

Today, the abandonment to any considerable extent of national sovereignty is something which in practise no people will permit. The forces against it are too strong, the arguments against it too readily acceptable. We must therefore find a way by which sovereign states of common interest can work together to the accomplishment of common ends; by which humanity, without drastic change in accustomed and familiar ways of government, can prevent its own self-destruction. Surely this is not too much to ask, or even to expect.

Ingenious and complicated plans for the future world have great appeal to many minds. But there is no permanence and little hope in any plan which cannot be readily understood and made their own by the great masses of the people of the United Nations, which cannot have a common and irresistible appeal to the average man and woman throughout the world. Statesmen may draw up wordy documents; presidents and prime ministers may affix flowing signatures beside beribboned seals; but it is in the hearts of the millions that the only reliable and permanent foundations of peace can be established.

It is these millions who have purchased victory at the price of their blood. It is these millions who must see to it that they are not cheated of the fruits of victory.

However sound the work of our planners, however noble the purposes of our leaders, these plans and these purposes must become the plans and the purposes of the people before they can endure. One of our greatest tasks is therefore that of education. Not education from the top downward, not the education of the Ministry of Propaganda and Public Enlightenment, but the education which comes from thought, discussion, argument among folk in every walk of life. The task of government in this sphere is not to teach, but to stimulate discussion; not to issue hand-outs, but to encourage an active popular interest in the formulation of policy. A free press, a free radio, the motion picture, the lecture platform and the mass meeting, political debate and learned research are all instruments which aid in this process. The makers of war must be taught that free peoples possess in their very liberties the indestructible ingredients of self-protection. As Elihu Root once put it, "When foreign affairs were ruled by autocracies or oligarchies, the danger of war was in sinister purpose. When foreign affairs are ruled by democracies, the danger of war will be in mistaken beliefs. The world will be the gainer by the change, for while there is no human way to prevent a king from having a bad heart, there is a human way to prevent a people from having an erroneous opinion."

When free men and women everywhere come to realize that their security depends on preventing those of sinister and secret purposes from possessing the means to attempt execution of those purposes, the foundations of a people's peace will be well and truly laid.

12. AMERICA'S DESTINY

It remains only to examine, from the point of view of American interests and American security, the implications of the suggestions heretofore made for the establishment of a lasting peace.

It should be clear to all thinking men that military policy and foreign policy must go hand in hand. The nature of the one is determined by the requirements of the other; and the scope of foreign policy cannot go beyond that which military resources can support.*

The foreign policy of the United States must be either one of cooperation with other states for the achievement of objectives common to all, or it must be one of attempting to achieve American objectives without such cooperation.

In the former case, it can seek objectives of far wider scope, for its policy can be supported by the whole of the united military strength of all cooperating nations; in the latter case, American policy must be limited to objectives which can be supported by the military power of the United States alone.

The first policy seeks by active measures to make friends and to keep them; the second regards all the world as potential

* For a further discussion of the principles involved, see "The Ramparts We Watch," Chapter IV; also "U. S. Foreign Policy," by Walter Lippmann.

enemies. The first is the policy of growth and life; the second the policy of stagnation and paralysis.

In the military sense, the first policy is offensive in principle, because it seeks to prevent the arising of threats to our safety by dealing with the symptoms of such threats before they become great enough to endanger us; the second policy is defensive in principle, because it deals only with danger after it has grown great enough to approach our shores in tangible form. It should be noted, that in military considerations the offensive principle is the vital principle which alone can give decisive results; the defensive principle is adopted only by those who have no other choice, and is the inevitable forerunner of defeat unless it can at some subsequent point be translated into the offensive.

Therefore it may be said, with all the force of axiomatic truth, that the military policy which must go hand in hand with a foreign policy of cooperative effort to maintain peace, is that which in all military history has been essential for victory; and the military policy which must go hand in hand with a foreign policy of isolationism is that which has always meant either defeat, or victory bought at unutterable sacrifice.

There is further to be considered the geographical factors which have to do with military policy. The military policy of an insular state must always be an active and in principle an offensive policy, because the insular state must, in the nature of things, retain command of its sea approaches and be able to use the sea (and, today, the air) for its own purposes if it is to retain the advantages of its insular position. These advantages are, first, the freedom from fear of imminent invasion by great land forces, which dispenses the insular state from the need for maintaining huge conscript armies and enables it to concentrate its military expenditures on its fleet and its air power; second, the political freedom of action which comes from always having a time factor in its favor, so that it may choose its course of action with deliberation instead of having a course of action suddenly thrust upon it by the deliberations of others; third, the military freedom of action which enables it, as the United States is doing today, to throw its military weight against the weakest part of the enemy's positions, to choose its own battlegrounds and the conditions under which it will fight; fourth, the economic freedom of action which comes from its ability to draw on the resources of distant lands for its supplies, and to deny those resources to its enemies.

It was the exploitation of these advantages that enabled the British to maintain the balance of power in Europe which was the central pivot of the Pax Britannica. It is in the exploitation of these advantages that the United States, an insular power in the military sense, must seek to preserve the security and peace which Americans are now fighting to establish. But it should be apparent to anyone that these advantages can be retained today only by an active policy which includes not only command of the sea but also of the overseas airlines by which the continent of North America may be reached from other continents; and that it will not be enough merely to establish a wall, or an outpost zone, or an imaginary line of defense drawn on the surface of the oceans, and outside that area to abandon all initiative to potential disturbers of the peace.

In fact, we must go farther than the mere statement of advantages; we must see how these advantages are to be applied to the conditions which will confront us. We have the advantages, as Britain had them in the century following Waterloo. How did Britain use them?

She used them, consistently, to prevent the accumulation of dangerous aggregations of hostile power on the shores of continental Europe opposite to the British Isles.

To be more precise, she used them to prevent any one power from becoming paramount in Europe; therefore, British sea power, and the influence which that unchallengeable power gave to British diplomacy, and the strength which it gave to British commercial and financial operations, were steadily employed against the expansion of whatever European nation happened for the time being to be most aggressive, and to show signs of desiring domination of its neighbors; and was just as steadily employed to support whatever continental power or powers might be threatened by this aggrandizement, which powers became, for the time being, the almost automatic allies of Britain.

This is a policy of action. It is a policy of eternal vigilance. It is a policy of the offensive against danger in the making rather than of defense against danger full-armed and on the march. How different would have been the history of Britain, and of the world, if the British people had adopted the defensive policy, if they had sought to be "impregnable" to attack, but had abandoned the political and the military initiative to those who might wish to attack them; if they had said, "We are secure behind our sea walls; let our enemies come over here if they want to fight, and a million Britons will spring to arms between sunrise and sunset to fling the invaders from our shores. Meanwhile we will have nothing to do with the eternal quarrels and hopeless hatreds of the continent."

It is quite true that for a time America has been secure against foreign attack by reason of her distance from sources of possible peril. But it must not be forgotten that our early statesmen were fully aware of these principles of sound policy. They saw to it that there should be no accumulations of dangerous foreign power within striking distance of our shores; they did not rest until the Spanish were driven from Florida, until the French were out of Louisiana; and finally they adopted the Monroe Doctrine which—as long as it had the support of the British fleet—prevented any further establishment of foreign military strength within this hemisphere. There can be little doubt that had anything happened to weaken the British sea power, we should ourselves have immediately commenced the creation of a powerful Navy, just as we did in fact finally do when the growth of the German fleet threatened the sea supremacy of Britain, and the growth of the Japanese fleet gave us a new and formidable foe upon our Pacific sea frontier.

But we were in those days tied to the old traditions of isolationism. Our foreign policy did not keep step with our military needs and with the change in the military conditions of the world. We did not, as we should have done, seek alliances with those of like interest, and we did not, as we should have done, seek to prevent the accumulation of dangerous aggregations of power on the shores opposite to us. We were still bemused by the illusion of the protection of distance, when in fact that protection was visibly shrinking almost day by day. We pursued a purely defensive military policy, and we found a defensive or at least an unfruitful, uncertain and hestitant foreign policy thrust upon us because we were unable or unwilling to provide the necessary support for a more active one.

It was not idly that Lord Nelson once remarked, "The sea frontiers of Britain are the shorelines of Britain's enemies." That is the basis of the true policy of the insular power, then and now and always.

But the conditions in which that policy must be exercised are widely different from those which confronted the Britain of Nelson's day, or the America of the 19th century.

The conditions are, as we have seen, a world in which there will be only three great military powers: America, Britain and Russia. These powers will, when victory is won, have succeeded in defeating and disarming two other powers of great military potential, Germany and Japan. One other nation, allied with the first three, may in time become a great military power—China.

Now the policy of the United States must be either—(1)

to regard all other states as potential enemies, in which case the supporting military policy must be to build up enormous defensive strength, to be prepared for any eventuality, to enter upon an armaments race with Britain and Russia, and therefore not only to take upon our people the crushing financial and economic burdens of such procedures, but to throw away the goodwill and the hard-won mutual confidence which is now proving so valuable an instrument of victory, and to insure that, by reason of the lack of unity among the victors, the defeated nations shall rise again to dangerous strength and be enabled to embark upon a war of revenge; (2) to seek unity of policy with Great Britain only, which brings about almost the same results because it means an armaments race between America and Britain on one side and Russia on the other; it means rivalries and uncertainties; it means the eventual seeking of one side or the other for the support of the Germans and perhaps the Japanese; it means an inevitable attempt by the Russians to expand into the spheres of sea and long-range air armament, and in the end it means another war; (3) to seek unity of policy with both Britain and Russia, within the framework of a general political unity of all the United Nations, which means the combination of all the available military power in the world for the attainment of ends common to its possessors, which permits the reduction of armaments to reasonable levels without loss of security, and which means the continued disarmament of the aggressor nations, Germany and Japan, and the peaceful growth of China and the rebuilding of the lesser nations in a world whose peace is maintained because there are none with the strength to break it, or to dare to think of breaking it.

Our choices, therefore, are clear. We can go it alone; or we can team up with Britain, excluding Russia; or we can seek to form a tri-partite agreement which will embrace all three, and try to make it permanent. Which policy affords most of hope for the future, and promise for our children? It is a question which hardly needs to be answered in words. The answer is self-evident.

There is neither external nor internal security in mere defensive armament. If it is to be of even temporary value, it must be enormous; probably so enormous that its mere maintenance will cripple the finances of the state and impair the foundations of our democratic institutions. No free people can make total war today without temporarily surrendering, as we and the British have been compelled to do, a great part of their cherished liberties into the control of the executive. Our democracy has been strong enough in the past to recapture those liberties when our wars have ended; but permanently to maintain a high level of readiness for war against any conceivable combination of foes in a world where we count none as allies would be a course fraught with perils both economic and political. To prevent the accumulation of too much power in irresponsible hands is a wise external policy for free nations; it is an imperative internal policy for free citizens, and it must be recognized that the mere possession of power tends to create irresponsibility in its possessor. The whole political tradition of the English-speaking peoples bears witness to this basic truth.

Nor can defensive armament, no matter how powerful, give us the security we seek against external aggression. This is not only because the defensive policy is militarily unsound; it is also because a defensive military policy means stagnation of foreign policy, and stagnation of enterprising and constructive thought on the part of those who adopt it. As John K. Jessup points out in the *Time* survey, *America and the Future*, "there was nothing militarily fallacious about the Maginot Line, as far as it went: the weakness lay in the Maginot frame of mind behind it." In fact, the building of walls on the frontier has ever been the sign of decadence in the people behind the walls. It was true of China, it was true of Rome, it was true of France, and it will be true of America if ever (which God forbid) we should likewise come to the wall-building frame of mind.

Indeed the strongest possible argument against the whole policy of isolation is that it implies a military policy which in this modern world is both foredoomed to defeat in war, and which prepares us mentally and morally for defeat before war comes. It leaves us helpless to take preventive action against accumulations of dangerous power, or to do anything at all save to cower behind our defenses and await the strokes that will surely come in the end. The world has grown too small for this policy to be of service to any state, least of all to a great power.

For the hard fact is that in the world as we will find it after this war, it is no longer a matter of Britain's preventing the accumulation of dangerous power on the continent of Europe, or of the United States preventing the establishment of hostile bases in the Western Hemisphere. It is rather a matter of all peoples who would be free, independent and self-governing, having a direct and vital interest in preventing the accumulation of dangerous power in irresponsible hands anywhere in the world. That is what modern techniques of war-making require today's statesmen to provide against. Nothing less will serve the purpose of any free people. And since no one of them can do this task alone, the responsibility lies on their governments to find means of doing by joint action what individual resources are unequal to accomplishing.

The principle is the same as the principle of the Pax Britannica or the Monroe Doctrine; but the field of necessary preventive action has extended to the whole world, rather than to a single continent or a single hemisphere. What is required now, in the words of Woodrow Wilson, is "not a balance of power, but a community of power; not organized rivalries, but an organized common peace."

For America, this does not mean the abandonment of her historic freedom of action save by specific agreements for specific purposes, as her interests may require from time to time. In any case, the relations between the United States and each member of the United Nations will be governed by the conditions of the hour, and will vary in accordance with the policies and objectives of the other nations, and their incidence upon American interests. It is quite probable that in many ways our relations with the nations of the British Commonwealth will grow very close indeed; there is much broader ground for mutual understanding and close cooperation between the English-speaking peoples, with their historic devotion to the great principle of freedom under law, than there is between any of them and the Russians or the Chinese. Yet our differences with Russia are almost altogether ideological, and hardly at all political or economic; we shall have much more to adjust in the economic field with the British than with the Russians or almost anyone else.

The point is, not that we shall not have differences with one or the other of our associates, but that we shall all agree on the fundamental question of maintaining the general peace, and that we shall take such military and other steps in common as are essential to maintain that peace; and that above and beyond this objective, we shall provide an agency or agencies by means of which this common policy may be coordinated and administered, and through which it may be periodically reviewed and altered to fit the changing conditions which must inevitably confront us.

One of the most dangerous rocks upon which hopeful argosies of international cooperation have been wrecked, is the rock of change. It is quite useless to attempt to bind sovereign states to act in a manner which may, in time, come to be contrary to their interests, or to obtain the signatures of political leaders to commitments which their peoples will not allow them to fulfil when the time comes. Any policy which has the vital quality of life, of survival, must be a policy which admits of change to meet new conditions. The blueprints of the future which are so lightheartedly constructed by the thinkers of today have all, in general, this failing: they are attempts to foresee that future beyond the limits of human power to peer behind the veil. They place their faith in the written word, without insuring the acceptance of that word by the people whose blood and treasure must guarantee it. They seek to give the sanction of law to their plans, without realizing that law as between sovereign states is simply and always the law of the strongest, the law of survival, forever open to challenge by the sword unless defended by a sharper sword. We, who now propose to lay the foundations for a reign of law among all nations, must therefore not only see to it that our beginnings, in their tender youth, are defended by overwhelming military power, but that this power is kept invincible and united by providing for changes and adjustments to meet the needs of the nations which have joined together to create it.

In any rigid system there must inevitably arise frictions, minor at first perhaps but growing more dangerous with time, until our whole peace machinery may fly apart by centrifugal force after the framework which holds it together has become weakened by these frictions till it is no longer adequate to its responsibilities.

Let us remember that armaments are a means, and not an end. No people would for a moment bear the expense and the burden of armament, nor endure its perils to their domestic institutions, were it not that they need it to be secure against the designs of others on their liberties and their possessions, or that they themselves cherish designs upon the liberties and possessions of their neighbors. The basic reasons for armament are thus either security or change. We shall hope to see the vast bulk of the world's armaments after this war dedicated to the purposes of a common security for its possessors, none of which can be said to cherish aggressive designs. The total burden of such armament can therefore, with time, be somewhat reduced, because armament is relative and needs be sufficient only to meet what actual danger may be apprehended. But there must, if this happy state of affairs is to have any degree of permanence, be adequate provision for peacefully making such changes as may be necessary in order that no state may be tempted to seek such changes by force, or that any which is so tempted may be dissuaded by the very hopelessness of success.

Most Americans will be willing and more than willing to subscribe to these doctrines and to subject our own possible desires for change in the future to accomplishment by peaceful processes. Most Britons will be willing to do likewise. There are good reasons for supposing that this applies also to Russians and Chinese, as certainly it does to the majority—not all, perhaps—of the peoples of the lesser states. While these conditions continue to exist, we can have not only reasonable assurance of a peaceful world, but we can enjoy conditions in which we may usefully and hopefully plan for an even better world in which the approaches to a real world government can be begun: provided that we take advantage of these conditions and seek by due effort to preserve them.

This does not mean a weak America; it means a strong America. This does not mean a disarmed America, but rather an America vigilant to defend her rights, and armed to that purpose, that she may discharge her fair share of the responsibilities which she may enter into by agreement with her associates. It does not mean an America which must go to war to preserve the boundaries of every member of the United Nations; it means an America eternally vigilant against the conditions which lead to war, prepared at all times to cooperate with her associates to that end, and determined to prevent dangerous accumulations of power in irresponsible hands as the chief menace to the common peace.

It means an America devoted to the principle of freedom under law which has ever been the birthright of her people, and resolved upon the preservation of that principle and the gradual spread of its protection over all the peoples of the earth, great and small, that every human being may walk in dignity before his God, acknowledging no human master. It means an America resolved that the black curse of war, and the fear of war, must be lifted from the souls of all mankind, so that they may look unafraid upon the sun and be thankful for the fruits of the earth which are given to them in such abundance if they will but take them.

It means an America great enough and wise enough to hold out her hand to the other free nations of this world in friendship; to say, Come and unite with us in this sacred bond, and be prepared to support it with us. They who have taken the sword have perished by the sword. Now let us see to it, together, that the sword which has been the sword of victory shall become hereafter the sword of justice, so that our children may not perish but may live to enjoy the heritage which is their birthright.

We Americans alone cannot bring peace to the world. We can do so only in loyal cooperation with others. But we can make the greatest contribution of any people to the establishment of a secure peace if we will—the greatest material contribution and, I think, the greatest spiritual contribution. We are yet a young nation, an idealistic nation, a hopeful nation. We have suffered cruel disappointments because of these things, but we are still the hope of the oppressed and the fearful throughout the world. No American can travel in foreign parts without realizing how much of the hopes of common folk in every land are centered on this great free Republic of the West. If we are false to our responsibilities now, we shall in very truth break the heart of humanity. If we are faithful to them, we may lead the world to such an era of peace and of well-being as it has never known, and find our own peace, our own well-being, in assuring those of others.

It is for this great destiny that our nation was born. It was that America might be strong enough to fulfil this task that the Almighty placed us securely on this continent, hedged about by guardian oceans, until the hour of the world's need called us to rise in our might. It was for this hour of triumph and of trial that we have lived, prospered and grown strong. It is in this hour that we are called upon to be strong not only in material might, but in heart and spirit, that the freedom we have won for ourselves may become the heritage of all mankind.

This, under God, is America's destiny. Let us be judged by the manner of its fulfilment.

THE END

INDEX